THINGS I LEARNED
ALONG THE WAY

George Nye

ISBN: 9781075958236

Table of Contents

Preface

It strikes me as funny that in this reflection upon my life as a minister of the gospel, I start out looking like a fool and end the story with being called a Badass. Well, I guess that's just about right.

I preached my first sermon when I was sixteen years old, and to date, I preached my last sermon when I was eighty years old. I've heard, on a number of occasions, that I get paid quite a bit considering that I only work one hour per week, and that on Sunday mornings. Speaking to that issue, I consistently practiced what I learned in school, that I am to spend one hour of preparation for every one minute of preaching. I fully embrace a quotation by H.B. Charles, Jr.: *"A passion to preach without a burden to study is a desire to perform."* For me, preaching is a sacred calling through which I am to be a channel of blessing, instruction, and redeeming inspiration by being available to the Holy Spirit to accomplish God's will, not my own, in the pulpit.

Besides being the business manager of a Christian corporation, and the administrator overseeing a number of functioning employees, committees and commissions, what else does a pastor do with his/her time? What comprises his/her workweek, month in and month out? I don't pretend to answer for other clergy members, but this biographical memoir is written to give you a glimpse into this pastor's 50-60 hour workweeks. I have written this for your enlightenment, of course; but also, it has been written to inspire you and to share with you times of both humor and heartbreak, struggles and victories, that have typically marked my life as one who was called by God to serve in His earthly kingdom work over a period of nearly sixty years.

It has also been written to bear witness to divine interventions of our loving Lord that have come to me and my family in a variety of ways through the years, and to encourage you to look for the divine interventions that have come to your life as well.

George Nye

1

A Divine Intervention

ON ONE OF THE OCCASIONS in my life when my foolishness got my family and me in trouble, I'd decided to take the family on a Sunday afternoon drive, on a sunny day in February. We had moved from Seattle to Pocatello, Idaho, in August. I had accepted the position of pastor of the First Baptist Church in that city. When we got used to it, we gloried in the seemingly endless sunshine days in eastern Idaho, after years of cloudiness in Seattle. But then came fall and winter. The temperatures plunged to several degrees below zero for days at a time, freezing even the ground to a depth that caused cemetery workers to postpone burials until spring.

On that early February Sunday the sun came out and warmed the air. So after church I suggested that we go for a drive in the country to break out of our winter blahs. I still had my suit slacks on, and wore a light jacket. Our six-year-old daughter and three year old son shed their parkas for light jackets, as well, as did my wife, Sandy. We'd head for American Falls, cut across the edge of the desert to Blackfoot, and return to Pocatello. Shortly after we crossed the Snake River, I saw a sign pointing to the Crystal Ice Caves. *"Hey, why not take a quick detour out to see those ice caves?"* I turned onto that road where blacktop soon became gravel, and gravel became dirt. Not quickly enough, it became apparent to me that we didn't belong out there; but there was no place to turn around without getting stuck in the mud. By now I was driving through mud several inches thick. *"Ahh, there's a flat, wide spot down there where I can turn around."* Only I couldn't do so. *"Okay, I'll try that place, a little further out."* By now, we were three or four miles, plus, off the highway. Finally, a road came in from the left; that looked more solid. The sun had warmed and melted the top dirt, turning it into a thick layer of "slickery" mud covering the frozen ground. That mud was now nearly up to the doors and too slippery to drive in. Even more concerning, the mud was up to the tail pipe, making it too dangerous to idle the engine, while not moving.

With the afternoon sun heading toward the horizon, our light jackets would not get us through the night. Leaving Sandy and the children in the car, I headed back to the highway to find help, walking in the deep ruts, our tires had made. Never have I prayed more earnestly for God to send help than on that trek. After about a half mile of walking, I looked up, and there, coming toward me, was a Volkswagen Beetle, bouncing down the road. *"Lord, I prayed for help! And You sent a VW Beetle?!"*

The driver stopped to see what this obvious "greenhorn" was doing, walking along this mud-strewn road. I explained my predicament and he told me to get in and we'd go take a look at the problem. In the back seat were his two boys, about nine and eleven. The driver said that he had no idea why he was out there. He was watching a ballgame, and suddenly, his boys insisted that they have to go rabbit hunting. *"So here I am; but I don't know why I'd give up that game to come out here to go rabbit hunting!"*

I told him that I know why he's out here. At the intersection we got out and walked, each in one of the tire ruts, to where my big, 2-ton, '68 Ford Galaxy was sitting. He sized it up and told me to stay on the driver's side, he'd be on the passenger side, and with my wife behind the wheel; she'd put the car in reverse and softly touch the accelerator. As the wheels barely turn, we'd push the Ford sideways, back and forth, working it back to the intersection, where we'd shove the back end around until we lined up the car with the road out of there. In that amazingly slippery mud, it worked beautifully.

I thanked him profusely. He got back into his VW and headed for home; he didn't go hunting at all. I sat in the driver's seat for a moment to get my wits about me before driving us back to the highway. That's when Sandy said, *"Look at your pant legs."*

"What about them?"

"Look at them. There is no mud on your pant legs."

She was right. I'd been walking in mud six to eight inches deep for a half a mile, and pushing that car back and forth thru the mud, standing outside the ruts, for the equivalent of a city block, and there was no mud on my pants, nor was there any mud on the tops of my wingtip shoes.

"That's not possible!" We concluded that, no, it's not. That has to be the Lord giving us a sign that He was watching out for us.

I looked up that man's address. He lived only about eight blocks from our home. On Monday, after a frigid Sunday night, I bought a big box of chocolates as a thank you gift and took them over to him, after dinner. As I thanked him again, he said, *"I still can't figure out why we went out there. After I helped you, I just drove home, and the boys didn't even complain that we didn't do any hunting."*

"As far as I'm concerned," I said, *"you went out there because we were going to need help. The Lord sent you, and I'm deeply grateful."* My mudless pants and shoes – a second intervention – proved the point, beyond any doubt, to Sandy and to me.

2

God's Differing Ways
of Answering Prayer

BUT NOW, A SERIOUS CAUTION: Does that mean that my family and I get a free pass in life? Does it mean that we're privileged to live a "charmed" life in the Lord, and that we are more favored, more deserving, somehow more blessed by God, than other folks? Absolutely not. It most certainly does not mean that I can continue going through life, living foolishly like a spoiled child who depends upon my heavenly Parent to save me from my carelessness and lack of common sense. No universal truth can ever be extracted from a particular gift of grace. And so, **a learning**: As E. Stanley Jones put it, "*God gives us just enough miracle to strengthen our faith, but not enough to make us lazy.*"

To prove the point, about fifteen years later, that same son who was saved from the desert, graduated from high school. He didn't know what he wanted to do. He didn't want to get a job or go to college, so I told him to go up to our church camp near Mt. Hood, Oregon, and volunteer his services for the summer while he works out his next step. He'd worked in church camps before and liked that idea. Six weeks later, he ran down the boat ramp at Trillium Lake, did a shallow dive, hit his head on a traction bump, and broke his neck. He floated to the surface paralyzed from the nipples down. He'd also lost his hand function and half of his arm function; his biceps worked; his triceps were paralyzed. Over the next eight months, he went through numerous surgeries, recurring massive infections that included a toy football sized infection in his neck that tore open his esophagus, several near death experiences, and all of the emotional struggles that such a severely damaged person must endure. Literally thousands of prayers went up across the land for Mike's healing. But, though other families' loved ones were healed of paralysis during that same period of time; Mike's body was never restored. Some people were so frustrated by that "non-answer" that they blamed me for my supposed spiritual failures that blocked God from answering their prayers; so they left the church which I served as pastor. That was one of the most painful moments of my professional life.

Does God answer some prayers and not others? Perhaps, but not in the way that they were asked in this case. Thirty-three years later I look back and say, "*God did answer those prayers. He said 'No.'*"

We humans were looking at a very specific tragedy that must be rectified so that this young man, with most of his life ahead of him, can live out his years with a fully functioning body. "*Lord, repair those crushed vertebrae and heal that severely damaged spinal cord so that this quadriplegic person can walk again.*"

God looked at Mike's overall life and, in essence, said, "*No. I'll leave him paralyzed. The spirit is more important than the body. I can work better with what he truly needs in that paralyzed condition.*" Perhaps it's somewhat akin to the Apostle Paul praying multiple times for God to remove a *"thorn from his flesh,"* so that he could better serve the Lord. However, God's response was something to the effect, *"No, I think I'll leave that thorn there. You're more useful wounded, than you would be, were I to remove that which is wounding you"* (see 2 Corinthians 12:7-9).

In hindsight, we saw that even as the accident was coming toward him, Mike was being prepared for what was to come. As he continued to drift from his faith base in spiritual rebellion, through the summer, a young man, who was a missionary to an African country, came to be the featured speaker for a couple of weeks of camp. He connected with Mike and played a key role in Mike's spiritual turnaround in the days leading up to that daytrip to the lake. On the evening before his accident, Mike prepared a bedtime devotional that he shared with his cabin boys in which he told those boys that if he were to become paralyzed, he could handle living in a wheelchair with God's help, just as long as he could have his hand function. Where did such an illustration as that come from?

Mike had a defiant spirit within him from the day he was born. It first showed up when, even as an infant, he did not want to be cuddled. He would stiffen his limbs and arch his back to keep from lying relaxed in my arms. In his middle school and senior high years, that defiance caused a number of problems at school and in the neighborhood that affected his ability to live in community and set creative goals for himself in preparation for his adult years. At the same time, that spirit also gave him a heart for those who were in trouble, who were isolated, or needed a friend. He had the ability to touch the lives of others who lived out around the fringes, in positive ways that others of us could not. As a Cub Scout leader, he taught the boys that folks in wheel chairs are quite normal, except that they move around differently. He taught his niece and nephew the same lesson. During his employment days at Home Medical, customers stood in line for him to wait upon them, because they felt that he'd know, better than the able-bodied sales folks, about the equipment that they were seeking for their own family members with broken bodies. So when people became upset that I brought him home in a wheelchair, instead of the two of us walking together, I realized that, for myself, if I had to choose, I'd rather have a son with a broken body and a healed spirit, than a son with a healed body and a broken spirit.

The number of experiences that came my way as a pastor which resulted from issues surrounding Mike's injury, transformed and broadened both my pastoral and counseling ministries. This brought blessings, encouragement and insights into the needs of others, which I'd never have achieved without first going through my own suffering and struggles. For example, when Mike was struggling for a long time in various medical facilities in Portland, Sandy and I took turns making the 600-mile round trip from home to be with him. At this stage of his healing, I would go up to Portland for three days to be with him, and then come home for four days to be pastor of the church. During those four days, Sandy would go north to be with Mike, then come home to be away from all of that stress and pain, and to put in a couple of days of work at the bread store. It was not uncommon for us to meet at a

McDonalds, at the half way point between Medford and Portland, to check in with each other and exchange notes as needed, as we'd pass each other on I-5. There were also a number of weekends when our newlywed daughter and son-in-law, Linda and Andy Tripp, took some shifts to relieve us. (Over time, we noticed how other patients, whose family members and friends did not come to be with them and help them with simple tasks and therapeutic activities, did not thrive as well as those patients who daily received comfort and encouragement from loved ones.) They also contributed to the "buckets of tears" that were shed during those days, which turned into months. This was a serious commitment on their part, given that they were not only a new bride and groom, but Linda was also a senior, trying to finish up her college work and earn her teaching certificate as well.

One Wednesday evening, I showed up at the church midweek supper, ready to lead the Bible study later. I was weary and discouraged. A man across the dinner table from me asked how Mike was doing. I told him that Mike was doing okay for the moment, "*but I'm not doing so well.*"

His response was, "*Well, I guess there's always somebody worse off than you are.*"

I nearly went over the table for his throat. Then I thought better of it when I visualized the next day's newspaper headlines: *"Pastor Strangles Church Member!"*

Instead, I went silent and began reflecting on what he said. If what he said was true, as countless others have also said in some poor attempt to put all things into perspective, then on this whole planet of seven billion people, there is only one poor schmuck who is so bad off that the whole world must feel sorry for him, and him only – because there's no one worse off in all humankind than him. "*That's Just Plain WRONG!!*" I screamed in my head. It doesn't make any difference if there are other people in the world who are hurting more than I am. Right now I'M hurting. And I have a serious need to say so, to claim it, and to admit it to another person who has an obligation to hear it without judgment.

Out of that brief exchange came **two critical learnings**. The **first** often shows up in a hospital when I'm making either a pastoral or a chaplain, call. The patient in the bed will say something to the effect, "*Oh, Pastor, I know there are people here a lot worse off than I am, so I know I have no right to complain; but I hurt so much, and I'm so discouraged.*" And now I could say, with confidence, "*It doesn't make any difference what other peoples' painful experiences are. Right now, we're going to focus on your pain. We're going to honor the reality of it, and talk about your suffering, and your need for an extra measure of God's love and help.*" At this point, she/he has a companion on his/her journey of pain who hears her, who cares about him. And that is reassuring knowledge to the suffering person, who knows for a certainty that she matters, and her suffering is important.

The **second** critical thing that was reinforced for me was that there's more than one suffering person in that hospital room. There's also the caregiver, the spouse, the child or other family member who is quietly suffering over against the wall, or in the chair. I call them the "*Invisibly Injured.*" Everyone comes to see the patient and ask how he/she is doing. But most visitors pay scant attention to the person over against the wall. I'd play over in my mind, when I was over against that wall, the inferences I would get when I might say, "*He's doing okay for the moment, but I'm not doing so well.*" The inference in the response of the visitor would be, "*What have you got to complain about; at least you can walk!*"

That loved one may already be dealing with that very kind of guilt – illogical as it is. Such a challenge from a visitor does nothing whatever to ease her/his pain. So from that Wednesday evening on, I learned always to check on the patient first. Then, after an appropriate time, I will go over to the loved one, focus totally on her/him, and say, "*Now, tell me how you are doing, and where you are hurting.*" And then I'd listen for the answer. I could only have theoretically known that if I had not been that person in need at that church dinner. That man gave rise to a significant new feature in my overall ministry, for which I am grateful.

In **another learning**, I realized that neither Mike's injury, nor that church member's callous remark, was God causing a tragedy in order to give me an advanced degree in human pain and suffering. It's more to the point that in God's economy, nothing is wasted. It's, above all, the message of the cross, with God saying, "*Okay, bring all your hatred here, your false pride, your arrogance and willful ignorance. Bring your self-serving actions and desires, your mean-spirited actions toward those who oppose you. Pile it all up here, and we'll call it Mt. Golgotha. Is that all you've got? Oh, wait, there's some selfishness over there, some lust and orneriness. Bring it all here and throw it on the pile. Now, I'm going to put a cross on top of that putrid mess and use that very stuff to demonstrate My redeeming love for you, through the* *death and resurrection of My beloved Son. Your very action of killing your Messiah is what I will use, through My grace, to save you into eternal life, if you'll let Me. For that is how much I love you."* Apart from Mike's own journey through this catastrophic experience that had descended upon him, I was also on a journey of learning and awakening that would not soon be completed.

In my second pastorate, Maude Knapp was the last living charter member of the congregation. By the time I knew her she was in her nineties. One day she told me that she still rues the day that she demanded that God save the life of her son, about 40 years earlier. God answered her prayer as she prayed it. That son came back to life; but he was a very different, very much more unpleasant person than he was before his deadly illness. Maude lived with that heartbreak from that day forward. Everyone in Maude's family would have been better off, including the son, had he died that earlier death.

That memory came back to mind a few years ago, when a young father with three kids and a wife, lingered close to death in the ICU. When he coded, the nurses rushed in, worked their "magic," and finally got his heart beating again. Because of the detrimental nature of this man to his family, in my mind I was saying, *"Let him go. Let him go."* They "high-fived" each other at their success when his heart started beating again. I could only think, *"What a foolish thing to accomplish."* And sure enough: he came back such an abuser that the seventeen year old son had to defend the other kids, and his mother, from his father's mean-spiritedness. The family had to get a restraining order against him while the wife secured a divorce. I never heard that he ever returned to a manageable life. In my own experience, as well as

14

observing the experiences of others, **I've learned** that it is always best to express our desires to God, asking for the outcome that we feel would be best from our viewpoint; but then, recognize that it's equally important to ask that, from His perspective, God would accomplish the very best that He has in mind for this person or that situation.

In petitioning God with my own requests, **I learned** that prayer is not unlike counseling. In my counseling ministry, a theme of every new client is the attitude that *"I want the answer now! I want the problem fixed today!"* And my response is that an immediate enlightenment, an instantaneous transformation, is not possible. First, it typically takes weeks, months, occasionally a year or more, to unravel the problem to the point that the actual truth, the centering issue, can be discovered and faced. Second, the client is typically not ready to hear and receive the truth, along with its implications, until she/he has gone through a process of discovery, of gaining emotional maturity, and of getting other essential matters in place first. If I want a restored husband, am I willing to change my own life to accommodate that new relationship? If I want God to cure me of my addiction, my angry outbursts, am I willing to change my life and work at filling the void created by the loss of my addiction with healthy thinking and alternative activities? Am I willing to learn management and relationship building techniques to fill the void of my management by fear caused by my anger?

In the same way, I may not be ready to receive the answer I'm asking from God; or, perhaps I'm not prepared to implement that for which I am asking. A sequence of events must take place, or new insights must be embraced, before God can respond to my request. Acknowledging that such a thing may be the case, I will prayerfully state my petition. But then, my follow-up will be, *"If I'm not ready for the answer, then sustain me, Lord. Keep me from utterly falling until I am ready to receive the answer – until I've learned and accepted the thing I need to know."* For me, that latter part of the prayer is just as heart-felt as the opening petition. In the human dynamic of living, there are often a variety of sequences that must be put in place before God can act. In this personal predicament, I have learned that often times, the process of getting ready for the answer is far more important to my spiritual growth and understanding than the requested thing itself. For as is the case with counseling, or in the case of an agonizing circumstances descending upon a loved one, equipping the client to receive the answer may actually be preparing the client to live in several arenas of life rather than being confined to the one area that is so troublesome.

3

Our Value As Persons

IN MY RETIREMENT YEARS I'm a Court Appointed Special Advocate (CASA). I serve as an officer of the court. The judge assigns me children caught up in the judicial system through no fault of their own, who are most often physically and/or sexually abused, and victims of severe neglect. At the time of this writing, I've been holding this position for fourteen years. My job is to represent these children in court and, at the end of the day, recommend to the judge whether they should be returned to parent, placed in guardianship, or adopted out.

Though I'm not legally required to, I also work very hard with the parents to help them in their recovery and rehabilitation from their drugs and lives of crime. My feeling is that one of the best things I can do for the child I represent is to help return her/him/them to a rehabilitated parent. Occasionally, I will visit a mother in jail. At this point, she has lost her child; she has no sense of hope; she is generally ashamed, defeated, and despairing of any future for herself. As the jailer brings her to me, her eyes may be vacant, sometimes they're defiant, and her facial expression seems etched in stone.

As we talk for a bit, if the moment seems right and she seems vulnerable enough, I will lean forward, getting as close to her face as I can, with that wire barrier between us, and say something like this: "*Now you listen to me! You are a daughter of the heavenly Father, a child of the Most High God, in whose image you were created! And He LOVES you! And that makes you priceless. Don't you EVER forget that.*" And with that, tears usually begin to well up in her eyes, and her face softens, and life, remorse, hope begins to return to her face. And now, we can begin to move on toward a creative future. That is a moment in my life, which is also a priceless gift to me. What a wonder it is that God will allow me to participate in His work in that woman's life!

But wait a minute. Don't we Christians talk about being a child of God, being created in His image, conceived within the context of a fully committed love between our father and mother, and born into a warm Christian family, committed to, and according to, God's will? Ah yes, that concept is such a spiritually comforting and rewarding image, one that washes over us as the beloved parents bring their baby forward for dedication or baptism. That's certainly as our Lord meant it to be. However, most of the people I deal with, have been born, or have given birth to, babies that are the product of rape, sexual abuse, lust, drug abuse, rebellion or boredom. Occasionally, the mom is not sure which man is the bio-dad, without doing a DNA screen. When I consider the many stories of people whom I know, there is any number of us who should never have been born. In fact, I should never have been born.

When I look back through my lineage, I reflect on my grandfather's life (who was my role model for what it means to be a man). His mother, my great-grandmother, had an encounter with her second cousin, a man a generation older than herself, and she got pregnant. He wanted no part of that, so he abandoned her. Another young man stepped in to marry her and give my grandfather a name. (Being conceived out of wedlock in the late 19th century was a terrible social burden to bear, and had a profound influence on my grandfather's image of himself.) But the bottom line is that my grandfather should never have been born, in which case, I would never have been born.

My grandmother was born to a farm family, the second oldest of several children, whose father was widowed. It fell to my grandmother, as a young teen, to be the surrogate mom and housekeeper, while their dad worked the farm. He found a spinster Christian missionary lady who was getting older and wanted a stable home life; and they married. Shortly after the wedding (all in good, Christian love and charity, of course), she told my fifteen-year-old grandmother that the house was not big enough for the two of them, and my grandmother had to get out. Since her dad did not stand up for her, she had to leave the farm and move to Portland. She had sewing skills that allowed her to earn a modest living as a seamstress. In church one Sunday, she saw the back of the head of a young man sitting down front. She told her friend she was going to marry that young man, which she did. However, if her stepmother had practiced her Christian Faith, my grandmother would have been allowed to grow up in the family home on the farm, and again, I would never have been born.

My mother and her brother were the products of that

union. My mother was a very bright person, but she struggled with mental and emotional instability, leading her to several bouts of mental illness during her life. She had a driving desire to earn her father's undying approval; but never felt that she received it. So in fist-shaking rebellion, she married a man whom her parents told her not to marry. That young man became my father. They were both good people, but they never should have got married. After a few years of major stress, during which my brother and I were born, they divorced – ultimately acknowledging what was evident from the beginning – that there should never have been a union between the two of them in the first place. But, of course, if they had both done the right thing – the Christian thing – and not married, I would never have been born. Can I truly be a child of God then, when my very existence is the product of three generations of sinfulness and rebellion? For that matter, how can we say of a person who is the product of a violent rape that she/he was *"knit together in my mother's womb . . ."* and was *"fearfully and wonderfully made . . ."* as the psalmist (139) put it?

I went to the Bible for answers and I saw that the twelve tribes of Israel, upon which the Lord God founded his earthly kingdom, was based upon twelve brothers, most of whom were conceived and born out of trickery, lies, jealousy, spitefulness and revenge. And I read about the atrocities of king David (God's favorite), who committed adultery, and then murder, to cover that adultery. He was confronted by Nathan's scathing parable, rebuking King David for his treachery (2 Samuel 12). Then, the product of David's sinful marriage to Bathsheba (born as the result of lust and murder) was Solomon, one of Israel's greatest and most blest kings, who was granted the privilege of building the first Temple to God, when his father was declared by God to be sinfully unfit to accomplish the task, himself. Beyond that, Solomon had a mind that contributed magnificently to the content of the Bible.

What am I to make of that? Later, I turned to the psalmist who captures our origins beautifully: "*. . . You made all the delicate, inner parts of my body and knit me together in my mother's womb. Thank you for making me so wonderfully complex! Your workmanship is marvelous – how well I know it. You watched me as I was being formed in utter seclusion, as I was woven together in the dark of the womb. You saw me before I was born*" (Psalm 139:13-16) Part of the glories of God's grace is that He can use that which was conceived in sin to bring glory and honor to His name, while He makes a gift to the world of a brand new person, regardless of the sins of the parents.

So what **learning** do I have in all of these quandaries? Many humans are born into, or as the product of, sin. And yet, in spite of human sin – careless actions and willful actions of harm – God's will is accomplished in that unborn little human. A new generation is born to help accomplish God's will . . . "*on earth, as it is in heaven.*" The miracle of life, of the initiation of a new life through the union of the sperm and the egg, are not the embodiment of sin. The offense lies with the moral chaos of the hosts of the components of a new life. The Lord will love us through our desolation into His glorious light; for we are indeed, children of the heavenly Father, sons and daughters of the Most High God; and He LOVES us; and that makes us priceless – even when that great truth must be announced to a broken woman in a jail.

4

My Childhood

MY BIRTH ITSELF was a portent of my life to come – a struggle to rise above the circumstances of the day. A woman had her medical clinic in a house on Albina Avenue, just north of Killingsworth in north Portland. My mother and I did our best to cause each other problems. I was being born as she went through a series of contractions, one of which shoved my eyes so deep into my head that the doctor later, just opened my lids and dropped the eye drops into the openings where my eyeballs should have been. (Fortunately, they returned to their normal place in their sockets, a short time later.) At the same time, I was tearing her up pretty badly, which would soon require a number of stitches to sew her up. To make matters worse, I was born with the cord wrapped around my neck, and my head was blue, which meant that the oxygen was being blocked off to my brain, which should have caused severe brain damage. To top it all off, my grandmother was present, and was quite vocal in her agitation with the doctor over the way she was handling the birth (which must have been greatly appreciated by that obstetrician). Welcome to the world, baby George; hopefully, it won't all be downhill from here.

I wasn't "baby George" for long. I was named after my two grandfathers, though my maternal grandfather hated his middle name, George, so much, that he had it legally removed from his birth certificate. Further, neither of my parents liked the name "George," so they gave me the nickname of "Buddy." I went through a bit of an identity crisis for the first years of my life being both George and Buddy. My Dad left town, and the family, before my brother was born on November 30, 1943; and he sent me a letter from a hotel in San Francisco. In it, he tells me that I am no longer "Buddy" – a child's name. So he begins, *"Dear George: I address you this way as you my son, are now a big, developed boy of whom I am very proud."* He goes on to say that I must now set the example for my baby brother, guide him through life, encourage him to do well in school, etc. giving me instructions on the role I must play in the family, and then ending with, *"you will fill in my shoes and become the man to look out for mummy and baby brother."* That's quite a role for a six year old to step into. Sadly, my mother also felt that she needed me in that role. As a result, much of my "carefree childhood" was quickly lost to undertaking adult chores and being the emotional support for a fragile mother, who did the best she could under the circumstances. By the third grade, I laid down the law to my extended family: *"My name is George! I shall no longer answer to Buddy;"* and that nickname began to slip away. I had enough on my plate without having to deal with one name at school, another name at home, and confusion in the midst of others who weren't sure how they should address me.

Growing up quickly was not an option. I prepared my

first meal for my Mom, who was sick in bed, when I was four years old. The menu was cocoa, hot canned beets, peanut butter on bread, and a dish of ice cream. Plus, I washed the dishes afterward, and asked her if she had any socks that needed mending. By the time I was six, it was my job to keep the sawdust-burning furnace cleaned out, after which it was my task to fill the hopper regularly with fuel. (This involved filling three bushel baskets full of sawdust, climbing up on the ladder, and dumping it into the hopper, and then lighting the fire.)

By the time I was six, I was riding the city bus around Portland. I'd get on the 39th Avenue bus at the end of the line, ride it about ten miles up to 33rd Ave., where I'd get off and transfer to the 33rd Ave. bus, and ride over to the dance studio to attend my weekly tap dancing lessons. (Mom was not hoping for me to be a star dancer. She was hoping that learning to tap dance would help me to learn to walk down a sidewalk without tripping on every crack.) Later, I'd ride the trolley twice a week downtown, walk three blocks to the Morrison St. street car, and ride it up to the Medical Arts Building to get my twice-weekly allergy shot at the doctor's office. I'd also ride back and forth across the city to Grandma and Grandpa's house.

Those were also the war years, so we had food ration stamps, limiting our purchase of various food products – assuming there were food items on the grocery store shelves to sell. With ration books in hand, I began doing some of the shopping while Mom took care of my baby brother. I also had to dig up the side yard to plant our "Victory Garden," which was strongly encouraged by the government as our patriotic duty, as well as an economic necessity, during the food shortage years. That was okay. It cut down on the amount of grass I had to mow with that old push mower, which had hand holds too high up the handle for me to use well. (I'd push the mower with one hand on the cross braces, down near the blades, and the other hand up the handle, a ways.) I got my first paying job when I was eight years old, selling newspapers to the shipyard workers and others at a busy bus stop on Interstate Ave at Shaver St. I sold each newspaper for a nickel and kept two cents per paper as my income. That money went to help in buying my clothes. With a few weeks off here and there, I basically continued working, mostly without a break, from that time forward for my and my family's financial support for the next sixty years.

My mother gave me the gifts of **three valuable learnings** during those years – each of which was life changing. **First**, there were those stressful early days/months/ years into the divorce when I'd receive impossible instructions from my Mom on what I could, and could not, do when I was with my Dad. Then, there were the regular child swaps between parents, and the inevitable parental conflicts that were waged over and through me. To give me what help she could think of, Mom sent me to Sunday school in a neighborhood Congregational church. My bicycle was my transportation. Again, she stayed home with my baby brother. (That church can still be seen on the eastside of I-5 [which was built many years later], up on a hillside near the Swan Island off ramp.) Then Mom decided that both Larry and I needed Christian men as role models in our lives, so she began taking us downtown to the large First Baptist Church. It was there that I made some life-long friendships, where I committed my life to Christ as my Savior, and where I dedicated my life to fulltime

Christian ministry. The church community, and my faith in Christ as both my Savior and my Lord, would be the foundation stone for my life. It would be my source of security and guidance through the stress of trying to live well in the midst of my broken family.

Early on, Mom's **second** gift to me was to teach me about tithing, though that wasn't her goal in her desperate struggle to keep us afloat. Money was always scarce. (The tap dance lessons, paid for by my grandmother, had long since gone away.) But at this particular moment, Mom's total financial assets dwindled down to fifty cents. She was overwhelmed with what she must do to keep the three of us going. She told me, "*Tomorrow is Sunday. We'll go to church and I will tithe this fifty cents.*" We did and she did. She put a nickel in the collection plate. That Sunday afternoon there was a knock on our front door. The man standing there said that he is a city bus driver. He has two little boys; his wife left them, and he needs childcare for these two boys while he's driving bus. A woman at the cafe down on Interstate Ave. knew my mother and sent him our way. The next day, Mom began a job that would give her several years of income. For me, it was a lesson learned about the importance of tithing as part of our commitment to God – a God who would provide for our needs. That lesson has stuck with me and has been practiced, with a couple of school year interruptions, for the past seventy-plus years. I have never practiced tithing as a smart business move. I have always counted it as part of my expression of gratitude and faith in the God whom I call Lord.

The **third** lesson came during a time when our income included my paper route money, Mom's childcare money, and occasional child support payments from my dad. There was a young missionary couple in our church who were trying to prepare themselves for service in India. Al was preparing to be a medical doctor, and was in an internship at St. Vincent's Hospital in Portland. They had very little to live on; but the wife felt that if she could make most of their clothes instead of purchasing them, it would ease the financial strain on their minimal income. Mom had an upright sewing machine, and a portable machine. She decided that we didn't need both of them. So, we would donate one to Dorothy. I'm not sure why they called those early day "half-ton" sewing machines "portable;" but Mom assigned me the task of lugging that thing, down onto the city bus, which took me to where I could transfer myself, and it, to the streetcar, which hauled us up to the northwest part of town where I could next, bang up my legs carrying it up two flights of stairs to their apartment. But, as my childhood muscles recovered and my bruises began to heal, I learned that even when we are poor ourselves, we can contribute something important to others in need. That not only solves a problem for another person, but gives us a sense of dignity and privilege as well.

5

A Call To Ministry

I DID MY FIRST SPEAKING on the radio when I was five years old. I was in the Bedell's display window, a women's department store on the corner of S.W. 6th and Alder, in downtown Portland. We were selling war bonds to help pay for the war effort. My next radio efforts came in the 5th Grade when my teacher, Mrs. Douglas, recommended me for participation in some radio dramas on the Portland Public Schools radio station, KBPS. I did well and developed a real interest in radio work from then on – which stood me in good stead years later when I was regularly involved in radio work in Pocatello, Idaho, Salt Lake City, and Medford, Oregon.

During my sophomore year in high school, we had a Career Day in which people from all kinds of job skills and work opportunities were present to educate us students on the nature of the job, what skills and education are required, and so forth. I attended the one on radio announcing, and soon figured out that a career in radio was not for me. Then I attended the session on being a caseworker for the Department of Human Services. Curiously, for a teenager's reasoning skills, I'm impressed with my thought processes. I heard about all the ways that a person can get into trouble and need help, and what the state welfare program can provide the client during difficult times. What came to my mind was that DHS was dealing with symptoms, when, if we're really going to change people for the better, we have to start with the cause, the spirit, and the person's relationship to God. Until people get right with God, they're not going to solve their daily problems on a long-term basis. Therefore, I decided I should probably consider some kind of church work.

These reflections at school began to mesh with what was happening to me in our high school youth group at First Baptist Church, Portland. When I started attending that youth group as a freshman, it included 40-50 youth who were pretty much out of control. The fiftyish spinster lady who served as youth director, had a good heart, but was clueless about how to catch the imagination of teenagers, much less control the youth. After a disastrous weekend retreat at a conference center on the Oregon coast that included drunkenness and fortunately, only a couple of pregnancies, the youth director was fired. They found the perfect replacement in a young man who had just returned from a tour of duty in the war on the Korean Peninsula, and was attending college on the G.I. Bill. He was a no nonsense guy with a strong Christian Faith, which had been battle-tested in Korea; and he had no time for teenage "horseplay." He took the job on the condition that he could eject anyone of his choosing from the church youth group. He was employed with that condition; and in short order he ushered a half dozen youths out the door with the instructions never to return. The remainder of us, plus those who joined the group as we went along, he molded us into a deeply devoted group of

Christian young people. In my high school class of 1955, in that youth group, five of us who graduated made our commitment to go into professional Christian ministry.

A couple of years later, good friend Wiley Kehrli and I discussed organizing a gospel ministry team, during our college summer break. The purpose was to travel to small Baptist churches around Oregon, as a self-contained unit. Our original intention was go to small congregations who might be financially strapped to give their pastor time off for a Sunday. With two young women who also joined the team, and an older married couple who could provide us transportation, act as chaperones, and provide us with an organist, we became something of a traveling road show around Oregon. We'd lead the youth in a weekend program; if helpful, we'd teach Sunday school classes. We would also prepare the entire worship service, providing all the music and the sermon for the morning. It wasn't long before we were invited to larger churches than we'd first visualized. Wiley's thinking was that since he and I were considering giving ourselves to a lifetime of pastoral ministry, including preaching week after week, we ought to have a taste of what that's like before we got too far down the road. I concurred; and after undertaking that adventure for two summer college breaks in a row, we both were more committed to fulltime ministry than ever. I was very much attracted to preaching. For Wiley, though he was the pastor of small congregations for a time, his more effective ministries were in the associate work of a local church, and then in the regional work of the denomination.

It was in that second summer that my ministry was narrowed for me, from general ministry to pastoral ministry, by a divine call on a Sunday evening in the sanctuary of First Baptist Church, Portland. We ended our summer by taking the evening service in our home church. Since the pastor didn't entirely trust me to do a proper job for a congregation this size, I learned at the last minute that he scheduled me to preach a "sermonette," then he would follow with an appropriate pulpit presentation after me. As I was standing about half way down the side aisle, waiting to be called up to the pulpit, I heard in my head, *"This is what I am calling you to do with your life."* When I was called up to the pulpit, the pastor was sitting in his chair behind the pulpit, prepared to give his message. I moved around in the pulpit enough that I forced him to get up and move out of the way. I continued on with a full sermon, and then gave an altar call at the end of the service. Twenty two people came forward that night, most to renew their commitment to their faith, a few to give their lives to Christ as their Savior and join the church. That was a spectacle that was not typical for that congregation; but I moved forward from that moment, with never a doubt in my mind about what my professional life was going to be. However, The Lord had much to teach me before I could be of much use to the kingdom work; and I must admit that not all of the lessons were easily learned. My personal growth in ministry went off on a much different track than I would ever have dreamed.

An **important learning** came my way my freshman year in college when I was pledging Sigma Chi Fraternity. It was our pledge class' job to build the homecoming display, in the rain, one night. About 2 a.m. we were wet and tired. Bill Joseph and I flopped down on the living room floor. He was a practicing and devoted Catholic Christian; I was an equally devoted and practicing

Baptist Christian. In those days there was a fair amount of friction between Catholic and Protestant groups. So why wouldn't we, as wet and tired as we were at 2 a.m., get into a theological debate? Before long, I was saying, *"the Bible says . . ."* and he would say, *"the Pope says . . ."* I'd say, *"forget the Pope, the Bible says . . ."* And Bill would respond, *"forget the Bible, the Pope says . . ."* I learned, that night, that no effective debate can be held if we don't have the same Ultimate Authority. Added to that, my Philosophy professor was right: *"Everyone's Ultimate Authority is a faith statement. It cannot be proved."* –all of which rendered our argument over which one of us is correct, useless. That lesson guided me through fifty years of ministry, especially in Utah.

6

Marrying A Minister
And a Devastating Injury

THE LOVE OF MY LIFE, and my marriage partner for fifty-seven years (at this writing), is Sandra Kay McCrory Nye. We met on September 6, 1961, and after a nine-month courtship, I graduated in Berkeley, California; and then we went to Robinson, Illinois to get married on May 6th, 1962, after which we packed up Sandy's stuff, our wedding gifts, my mother and best man, and headed west for our first church parsonage and job.

Sandy was born in Palestine, Illinois to a family very limited in material wealth, but rich in family connectedness in the rural farm culture of southern Illinois. She grew up in Robinson, population 7,000, whose claim to fame was being the home of Heath candy bars.

Her earliest memories include going to her grand-parents' and uncles' farms, and her dad going off to the Navy to serve on a small flat top carrier, during the latter days of W.W. II, while her mother ran childcare out of her home. Sandy spent a good share of her early life in the First Baptist Church of Robinson, and was active in all the things in which children and youth participated, in those days.

She had a calling to ministry, and in 1957, Sandy headed to Chicago to attend Baptist Missionary Training School, an institution that had a rich heritage of training young women for service as missionaries, Christian education directors, and church administrators. By the time she enrolled as a freshman, B.M.T.S. was coming to the end of an era that it had served well. As it turned out, she was the last student body president to hold that office, and her class was the last to graduate from that school.

In her senior year, Sandy signed on to travel by train around the northeastern United States to work in the Baptist camping programs in various states. She had also worked in a variety of local churches in Vacation Bible School programs. During the school year, she worked in the tenements of inner city Chicago. The thought of her climbing up those tenement stairs, stepping over drunks in the hall, still makes me uneasy. But at the time, she didn't think she was in any danger. Nothing's changed. Throughout most of our married life, she walks into the middle of violence and shootouts to see what's going on. In Salt Lake City it was to walk down to the street to see why a totally out of control man was trashing his car and trying to trash everything else on the street, in a violent fit of anger after driving into a sewer repair hole in the street pavement. In Medford, she walked up to the street behind our house to see what was going on with firemen and police officers who were using impact grenades with weapons drawn to try to flush out some drug dealers, who were hold up in a house, nearby. Actually, that's a tribute to her parents who brought her up in a loving, safe, and trusting world.

Ah, but there was one thing that would send her in the other direction in a heartbeat – rats! She developed an abhorrence of rats because she saw babies in those Chicago tenement houses whose faces and ears had been bitten by rats when they were in their cribs. The thought of rats curdle her so that she'll close her eyes when they're shown on the television screen. But in Seattle, when she saw a rat walking across our backyard where her babies played, she was out there with a hoe in a heartbeat, ready to do battle with that hated rodent. That mother instinct has caused her, time and again, to move to protect, confront, support her children, no matter how stressful the issues have been. That tenacity was evident again when her child broke his neck, and she was going to be there to get him the help he needed, whatever it took.

I continue to marvel, more as time goes on, that this young woman would trust me with her life. When she graduated from college, she decided that she wasn't ready to go looking for a job yet. So she and her good friend, Evie Brown, decided to head west to see what adventures they could find in a graduate school in California, known as Berkeley Baptist Divinity School. She caught my eye on registration day in the school library and I decided that I wanted to get to know her better. A couple of days later, the faculty and student body went on their annual retreat to Mission Springs Conference Center down near Half Moon Bay. There, during a recreation time, I got involved in a pick-up softball game, where I played in center field. She just walked out onto the field during the game and offered me a drink from her Nesbitt orange soda . . . and the rest is history. I walked her to her sleeping quarters that night; and, as I said good night, I told her that I felt certain we were going to get married. That was on September 6, 1961. On January 6, 1962, I proposed to her; she accepted, and on May 6, 1962, we got married.

The Lord had to be involved. Very soon in our developing relationship, I had to tell Sandy that I was "damaged goods," so that she could step away early on, if she felt that's what she needed to do. I'd entered into an earlier doomed marriage to someone I'd been dating for years. That marriage lasted a few months. I had supposed that I was achieving God's will, when in fact, I was serving my own wishful thinking and hoping. It was the darkest, most painful time of my life. And, it would affect my placement opportunities as a pastor, in the future. Now, two years later, to my great relief, Sandy chose to risk continuing on with our deepening relationship. Several months later, with an engagement ring on her finger, we were coming up on Spring Break in March 1962. With our love for each other growing day-by-day, Sandy and I boarded a Greyhound Bus together and headed for Hay, Washington, for my interview as a pastoral candidate. Here was an Illinois girl, attending school in the San Francisco Bay Area, now considering the prospect of moving, with her groom, to set up a home in the middle of the wheat fields and cattle ranches of eastern Washington, to do ministry in a very unfamiliar environment for both of us. What an adventurer she was!

Even before we got to the end of the school year, she learned that life with me could be a little different. Do you know anyone who can take perfectly good food and ruin it before serving it? My senior year in school, I was a student pastor for a wheelchair bound pastor in a San Francisco church. I literally did his "leg work." But that trapped me into having to eat Sunday dinners with his wife and him. His wife was amazingly creative in the kitchen. What could she do to those mashed potatoes, to give them a little zing? Ah, Of course! Take the can of a couple of weeks' of bacon drippings and grease, which she keeps in the fridge, heat it up and pour it over the top of the potatoes. Umm. Yummy! She couldn't think of anything for the cooked rice, one day, so she generously poured green food dye all over it, just to give it eye appeal. As a child, my mother strictly taught me about being polite to any hostess, and eating whatever was put on my plate, whether I enjoyed it or not. That training came in real handy for me during that year of Sunday afternoon meals.

But the best was yet to come. It would be our first Easter together, so I invited Sandy to go to San Francisco with me, for the Easter Sunday church service with dinner to follow at the home of the pastor and his wife. I also invited our good friend, Jer, who would be our best man at our wedding in Illinois, in another month. Our hostess had chosen to serve us a special delicacy: real down home headcheese. Her mother, who was from Mississippi, was there to help her. What a surprise: The San Francisco butchers didn't have any hogs' heads in the meat market; so they'd have to order one. When it arrived, mother went to the shop to haul it home; then, she and her daughter went to work on it.

Table conversation that Easter included our hostess telling, and demonstrating, how she popped the eyeballs of the pig out of their sockets, with her thumb. We wondered which of the delicacies on our plates included those eyeballs – because in headcheese, "nothing is wasted." Then, Jer got an even more peculiar look on his face, as he was lolling something around in his mouth. His eyes got bigger as he reached up and pulled a long, sort of a white tape out of his mouth. Mother clapped her hands and declared, *"Oh, look! He got the ear tendon!"* Sandy married me, anyway.

Though Sandy traded in her M.R.E. (Master of Religious Education) degree for a Mrs. title, that did not diminish her Christian ministry. In recent years we went to Hay, to revisit old friends and the community. The church, now closed for nearly 30 years, still has, in its library, a large plywood covered VBS book that Sandy constructed two weeks after we arrived there, penniless and six weeks away from payday. (What kept us going was a money tree that the congregation had for us at our reception.) She taught Sunday school, worked in the Hay Ladies Aid, led the Christian Education Committee, helped give direction to the youth work, and became choir director. Oh yes, and after a time, she got pregnant.

In 1965, three weeks after we arrived in Seattle, Sandy gave birth to our baby daughter, Linda. After she adjusted to motherhood, Sandy continued working in Christian Education, teaching a Sunday School class, giving leadership in Vacation Bible School, while singing in the choir. She also served as Chair of the Board of Christian Education, and worked with the American Baptist Women on an outreach project to provide a weekday ministry to neighborhood girls from the public housing projects that were near the church. One of the most popular classes was sewing. Our women taught the girls to sew on buttons, repair zippers, and fix tears in the cloth and seams that had come unstitched, so that they could wear clothing that looked nice, and made them feel good about themselves, while they were being taught useful seamstress skills. Years later we heard that that ministry was still bearing fruit up in Bellingham, Washington, where one of the girls in the Seattle program was so positively affected by that ministry that she started a similar program for girls in that city. It was also in Seattle that we welcomed into our family, through adoption, Michael David Nye, who was fifteen days old when we got him, born almost three years after his older sister, Linda.

In Pocatello, she added to her portfolio, becoming a Blue Bird and Campfire leader. She also worked as a citizen volunteer through the P.T.A. with School District #25, helping as an *ad hoc* negotiator during a terribly damaging teachers' strike. In Salt Lake City, she continued with the effective types of ministries that she has done so well for fifteen plus years, and added to her resumé – being a pre-school teacher – in the church's very effective and highly regarded pre-school program in that city. The majority of the children in the program came from Mormon families.

In Medford, Sandy added one more ministry to her resumé – a deeply appreciated ministry that has continued to grow in our retirement years. This is a card ministry with a personal note and thoughts sent to those who are grieving, suffering from illnesses and accidents, and to those who find themselves in difficult circumstances who can use an encouraging and reassuring word. This was added to her practice of giving crèche' scenes to newlyweds in the church before our retirement. She has been faithful and nurturing, touching the lives of numerous children and adults who have gone on to other things. Hundreds of people bear the contributions that she has made to their lives through the past fifty-six plus, years.

But now, there's another contribution, which Sandy has made to each church that we have served that is beyond measure. That contribution is her role as a pastor's wife – more specifically, my wife. Whatever kind words recipients of my ministry have had for me, whatever skills they believe I've demonstrated that have positively affected their lives, are attributable, not to me alone, but to Sandy, as well. A pastor cannot reach his/her full potential, or meet his/her daily responsibilities well, if he/she does not have the complete support of his/her spouse. When a pastor has to deal with marital stress, criticism and lack of support at home, while dealing with the stressful and demanding work at church, he/she cannot do well.

The church is a terribly demanding mistress. When someone is in the ICU, fearing that he's dying, he wants his pastor now, regardless of the pastoral family's needs! When someone is experiencing a mental breakdown at 2 a.m., she wants her pastor now, regardless of the disruptions to the pastor's family. (A pain that I continue to carry in my heart twenty years later, derives from a 10 p.m. phone call I got from a lonely woman in the ICU, who had no family support. She was afraid, alone, and wanted me to come and spend a few minutes with her. I was tired and it had been such a busy day. I told her I couldn't come, that evening; but I'd be sure to see her in the morning. She died a couple of hours later . . . alone. Morning never came for her.) Sometimes people want to be called on in their homes, and they're only available in the evening. There are numerous board and committee meetings that are called together in the evening that requires a pastoral presence. My ministry included an extensive counseling ministry and many of those clients needed to meet in the evening. Again, people never check the pastor's calendar before dying. Memorial services must be held, weddings performed, sermons and Bible studies written/prepared, and the pastor's wife is sitting home alone, night after night. Sometimes it's four to five nights per week. As alone as Sandy has been, never has she nagged me or complained about the time I must spend to do my job. That's part of her sacrificial gift to the congregations that we have served, which almost never gets recognized. More times than can be counted, she has given me as her personal and sacrificial gift to the people of the churches we have served, and to her loving Lord, as well. That is a ministry that she has performed which has to be celebrated by the angels in heaven.

In Salt Lake City, Sandy saw a sign in the Wonder Bread Store, advertising for a temporary store clerk during the Christmas holidays. She decided to apply for that job to earn enough money to give the family a Christmas gift of a train ride to Portland, a first for the children, and an opportunity to visit family. It was a wonderful gift; but as the new year got underway, her job was not terminated. So she decided she'd continue working because we had a daughter getting ready to go to college; and she would need all the financial support we could give her. When we moved to Medford, there was no Wonder Bread Store; but there was an Oroweat Store looking for help. She took the job and, over the years, she made a significant difference in our family finances.

When Sandy came home from work, our talk at the dinner table often focused on what she and her fellow employees, and her customers, had done or said, during the day. I have not been able to share with her, much of the most important things that have occupied my day, through the years. A pastor must carry the secrets of many people in his heart – their pains and problems, their sins and plans, hopes and disappointments. That means that just as the pastor cannot share those things with others in the church, neither does he share them with his wife. So through the years, it's not unusual that that which occupies the bulk of my attention and energy is the very stuff that I cannot share with my wife, which makes meaningful communication more difficult. But, even that, Sandy has understood, and has never complained. And, when she has been made privy to secret information, she knows how to keep it to herself and offer it up in prayer, but never to be a source of gossip. That is one more of her gifts of ministry to the congregation . . . that and her wonderful laugh. There is no pastor; there is no husband, who has been more truly blessed with a beloved mate, than I am blessed with Sandy.

Being a pastor and a parent has its own set of peculiar dynamics. On the one hand, being busy throughout the waking hours of the children, robs the family of that "quality time" we often talk about. It also bars the family from worshiping together as a unit on Sundays. On the other hand, it provides times during the week when the pastor can adjust his schedule to attend school events, when wage earning parents find it impossible to get time off, for their child's special moments. Though we never had weekends free, I was able to find weekdays to take time off when we did a lot of camping, hiking, canoeing, even when the children were small enough to fit into those new inventions called "Infant seats." We bought vacation property up on a forested lake in the Puget

Sound area, where we spent a lot of enjoyable time. We did a fair amount of tent camping in Idaho, and a lot of hiking the trails along the Wasatch Front in Utah, as the children grew up. Over the years of child rearing, we made a number of trips to Illinois, to visit maternal grandparents and a great many relatives. One of my favorite events, each year, was to be my daughter's date at her annual Father/Daughter dances, sponsored by the Campfire Girls. As to how effective I was in parenting, I'll leave it to others to say. My great pride and joy, throughout her life, has been my daughter. Her commitment to the Lord, her use of her musical talents to lead others in worship, her intelligence and her teaching and leadership skills, her parenting skills, and her partnership with her husband, have all brought lasting blessings to more people than can ever be counted.

The greatest single and sustained challenge to our marriage was our son Mike's injury. We went through eight months of surgeries, numerous near death moments, setbacks, tears and terminal exhaustion. Since he was hospitalized in Portland, nearly a 600 mile round trip on I-5, north of Medford, we took turns alternately driving up and back, to stay with Mike through his ordeal. Thanks to a church member's suggestion, West Coast Airways, later, gave us two free standby passes to fly the round trips, which made a big difference for us. A second major gift beyond price was the gift of a place to stay, while in Portland. Baker and Martha Brattstrom were friends of my mother, at First Baptist Church of Portland. I knew them, plus, I was a close friend of their son, Bob Brattstrom, who shared an apartment with me in grad school. Baker gave us their unused bedroom and bathroom upstairs in their home, and a key to the front door. Sandy and I took turns coming and going from that quiet retreat of rest and refreshment for the better part of a year, free of charge – with boxes of cold cereal in the cupboard, if we wanted a quick breakfast before undertaking the day. It's hard to express the depth of appreciation we have for that act of kindness.

Though it's not possible to describe, fully, what it's like to walk this journey, I still need to describe the "highlights" of that terrible journey, as best as I can, to help the reader understand what we parents went through in those initial years, following the accident. The first time we brought Mike home, close to five months after his accident, neither of us got more than three hours of sleep at a time, in the months he was at home during that first year. What three shifts of nurses and aides did during each twenty-four hour time frame in the hospital, we did by ourselves at home. It was a time of unending laundry, buying bottles of saline solution for his neck dressing changes, the gauze sponges, catheter tubes, syringes and needles for the IV flushings. It took thirteen hours to feed Mike each day, through his gastrostomy tube, which was surgically inserted into his stomach. One night, about 2 a.m., I found that his body had expelled that tube, sometime earlier, making a horrible mess in the bed. A huge, infectious mass on the end of that tube had to be cleaned off, and the tube disinfected. As it turned out, that mass was the unknown origin of what was poisoning his system and would have killed him. (Hospital personnel had searched for that infection source for weeks, to no avail.) So his body expelling that tube, turned out to be a life saving blessing. I called a local hospital, asked for a nurses' station, explained my situation to the nurse, and asked her to talk me through the process of reinserting the tube and securing it. Since the hole had already started closing, I had to tear some of the flesh open to get the tube back in place, before taping it over. It's amazing what we can do when we have to.

While still in the hospital, Mike needed to have a surgical procedure in his lungs. The problem was that he had developed allergies to morphine and painkillers that would put him into respiratory failure. When the doctor said that he must have a surgical procedure performed on his lungs without an anesthetic, Mike responded that he'd undergo it only if his Dad held him during the operation. It might have been a somewhat interesting experience for me, if the patient had not been my son.

The next major crisis happened when Mike's esophagus tore open. He had developed a massive infection in his neck cavity (the size of a toy football) that could travel down to his lungs, or up his carotid arteries to his brain. Either would have been fatal. Now, we had to learn to irrigate the interior of his neck cavity, through a long, open wound the surgeon had cut in his neck and left open. The surgeon could not stitch up that esophagus until healthy new flesh formed on its own, which would take months. In the present condition of that esophagus, the surgeon said that it would be like trying to stitch hamburger together. When we transported him from the Portland hospital down to Medford in a makeshift bed in the back of my station wagon, we then had to irrigate that open neck every three hours around the clock. In the meantime, Mike had fistulas that had opened up on his chest so that when he swallowed, the saliva, etc. came out on his chest that had to be continually cleaned up. His catheter and his uncontrollable bowels also had to regularly receive attention. When the sheets got messed up, one or the other of us, most often alone, had to clean him up and be able to change the sheets, with his paralyzed six foot one inch body still on the bed. (I was always amazed that "Mama Bear Sandy" could wrestle him around by herself. But she was up to the task every time.) Amongst other things, I had to be specifically trained to regularly irrigate the groshong tube inserted into his heart with the warning accompanying my instructions: *"If you make a mistake, you will kill your son."* Beyond that, of course, we both had to continue working at our places of employment.

The Lord had intervened in our lives in the Idaho desert when our lives were endangered. He had blocked me from unseen danger on the streets of Manhattan, and again in the forests of Washington State (which I'll explain, further along in this story of my life). And now, He intervened again at a vulnerable moment in my journey, a few days before Christmas. Mike had worked so hard in his physical therapy sessions to be able to get home for Christmas. We all were making plans for this great moment; but when his esophagus tore open, all those plans went down in flames. Mike was devastated, literally, beyond words. It was evening, and I was going to have to head for Medford the next morning, to prepare to lead a Christmas Eve service at the church. Mike had developed a place in his head where he could disappear, when reality became too painful or frustrating to bear. Mike was in that place, and I was learning how to catheterize my son. I was down in a mental hole, myself. I didn't think a Dad should have to be doing this to his eighteen-year-old son. Just then, some Christmas carolers came wandering down our hall, singing, *"Deck the halls with boughs of holly, fa-la-la-la-la, la-la-la . . ."* Then I could hear them coming our way with, *"We wish you a merry Christmas, we wish you a merry*

Christmas . . ." I couldn't stand it. I went over and closed the door against their music, and returned to my painful task.

A little later, all was quiet; the catheter was properly in place and hooked up to the bed bag; and the room was dark. I went to the window to stare out into the nighttime fog. Christmas lights were draped on the Rehab building across the street, and the colors of the lights drifted through the dark haze of the night. What could I say to my congregation? I was empty of words and hope. Then a voice came into my head: *"There were no colored lights on the buildings that first Christmas. There were no carolers in the dark streets to announce the birth of my Son. There was precious little hope to be offered to those townspeople on that first Christmas night. And yet, that's precisely the dark moment I chose to give you the gift of My Son."* With that message from the Lord in my head, my hope returned, my strength was rejuvenated – and, I had my Christmas Eve message all ready to go. Once again, I had been saved, this time, in a whole different context; but rewarding, refreshing, and reassuring, just the same.

After a couple of years in our home, Mike was stabilized, his throat had healed, and he acquired a specially equipped van which he could drive, and moved into his own home across town. He could not live alone without dependable attendant care, morning and evening, which was sporadic at times, non-existent at other times. Once he was up in his power chair for the day, he could move about at will. So when dependable caregivers were unavailable, his ability to life independently required attendant care from his parents, sometimes for a couple of weeks, sometimes for a year or more, at a time, plus a number of unscheduled "midnight runs" across town to clean up a mess, or change out a plugged catheter. Sandy and I took turns at responding to those phone calls.

After daughter Linda helped with Mike in the various Portland hospitals and rehab facilities, she and her husband Andy settled in the Rogue Valley, establishing a home and getting jobs. Linda also took some time to get her Mom away from the tension of daily life as a caregiver, and they hiked on some nearby trails. Once, Linda took Sandy to the coast for an overnight to walk the beaches and watch the waves and kite flyers. That was a therapeutic and bonding time for both of them, as adults together. It was during this same general time period that I received an invitation to join about twenty psychiatrists, psychologists and counselors from America to travel to the USSR to meet with our counterparts in the Soviet Union, and compare counseling techniques, both in the Russian culture of Moscow and Leningrad, and down in the Islamic culture of Uzbekistan, in the cities of Samarkand, Bukhara, and Tashkent.

Beyond that, the collateral damage done to Sandy and me, as his parents and his caregivers for years, strengthened our marriage, rather than destroying it. (Approximately 70% of all marriages challenged by such catastrophic events end in divorce. Some statistical studies move that percentage up to about 80%). Besides God's participation as a full-fledged partner in our marriage, we haven't analyzed what features we undertook to strengthen our union, save this one, which we identified after the crisis had passed. We never allowed ourselves to both be down at the same time. We never adopted the attitude: *"That's your job, not mine,"* or, "*I'm too busy – too tired – you'll have to cover for me.*" Oh, and one more: We never played the *"blame game."* When I'd see that Sandy was down, I had to stay up, to be in control and take the lead in accomplishing things that had to be done, until she recovered. And when she sensed that I was down, she stepped up and took control in the same way. When one of us needed to collapse, the other honored that and stepped in to carry most of the load for a time. That made us genuine and equal partners, and each, the one person whom the other could trust with his/her life and safety in her/his mate's hands.

I will sum up the miracle of Sandy in my life in this way:

- That she'd decide to attend school in Berkeley.

- That she'd go with my feelings that she was the right one, from day one.

- That she'd accept my painful past without question or a trial period.

- That she'd willingly say "Goodbye" to her homeland of the Midwest, its culture, family & familiarity, in exchange for rural Hay, Seattle, Pocatello, Salt Lake City, & Medford.

- That she'd willingly adjust to whatever income I could provide & make it work.

- That she's a woman of faith with a sense of calling to ministry and a sense of self worth and self-identity, which allowed us to be a valuable team to each church we served.

7

Lessons to be Learned
as a Young Pastor

AS A SENIOR IN GRADUATE SCHOOL, I can remember reflecting with my fellow seniors about the types of churches we would be seeking. I said, *"Well, I'm a city boy; I have to take a city church. I can't imagine how I would minister out in the country. I barely know which end of the cow to milk."*

What I didn't verbalize to my fellow students was, in my amazingly humble spirit, that I figured that I should probably start out being pastor of a two thousand member church, and work my way up from there. Twenty three hundred was the membership of my home church and, after all, I preached well in that pulpit, so I obviously was well equipped to begin at that level . . . *"Right Lord?"* What I learned, right off the bat was that the Lord has a remarkably perverse sense of humor.

My calling was to First Baptist Church, all right, but not First Baptist Church of Denver, Portland or Los Angeles. My call came to go to First Baptist Church, of Hay, Washington. More rural, I could not get. We were twelve miles from the nearest paved highway, out in the rolling wheat fields of the Palouse Country in eastern Washington. The church's membership was not quite as high as I would have hoped for – thirty-eight members, with a Sunday attendance of about twenty-eight on a good Sunday. And that was God's gift to Sandy and me – which was a bit hard to appreciate in the beginning.

Here, we unloaded our personal effects into the parsonage. The house was almost up to community standards; but it was so poorly insulated that the single circulating oil heater in the living room couldn't begin to heat the house properly. During the winter, the floors were so cold that Sandy's toes turned pink and blistered – the first stages of frostbite – from standing in the house on our floors. When she washed our clothes with her wringer washer, and hung the wash on the lines to dry, upstairs in our home, the first load would be frozen stiff, by the time she hauled the second load up those stairs. My study was cold enough that, even with an electric heater at my feet, that the postal stamp sponge on my desk would freeze solid. We could not afford a television, so we had to entertain ourselves with whatever was at hand. On some occasions, Sandy would grab the mop, I'd grab the broom, and we'd chase the mice around the living room floor to amuse ourselves.

The point is, that we really didn't know each other, when we got married. We were fulltime students, Sandy in her freshman year, I in my senior year; and, on top of the scholastics, I had to work as many hours as I could, selling shoes at Sears, to earn enough money to meet my current, and future expenses, that would come after graduation. We were absolutely chosen for each other. There was no doubt about that in my mind from the very first day we met, when she walked to center field to offer me a drink from her Nesbit Orange Soda can. But we still had to go through the business of getting to know each other intimately, socially, religiously, and as equal partners in this adventure called marriage, melded into a calling, which both of us had to ministry. If we had moved straight to that fantasy city church in my mind, even reduced in scale and size, we'd not have had the chance we had in Hay, to bond, to grow in love and dependence upon each other, to learn to survive creatively on a severely limited income, and to prepare ourselves for the life journey that stretched out before us. Just one example: Before we landed in Hay, Sandy had never prepared a meal. Her mother had never let her in the kitchen to do anything but wash dishes. So on our first day in the parsonage, she came into the study and asked what we should have for dinner. Knowing we'd bought a pound of ground beef, I suggested a meatloaf. Her next question was, *"How do you make a meat loaf?"* Since I had been cooking all of my life, I got her started in preparing meals. It wasn't long before she got the hang of it and took off, leaving me in the dust in food preparation and creating imaginative dishes.

Meantime, I started calling on my congregation. One day, I decided to call upon a hermit sister and brother couple who ran a rustic cattle ranch about five miles out of town. In the city, pastors wore suits and ties; so I supposed that that's how I should dress when I go out to make a pastoral call. I wore my only suit, a white shirt and a tie. First, after working my way up their winding, dusty, two-rut lane, I parked outside the barbed wire fence. I went through the gate. Then I literally pushed my way through about fifty head of cattle, watching out for cow pies. To get to the house I had to climb over another barbed wire fence, without snagging my suit trousers. Landing on the other side of the fence, I was greeted by three large, unfriendly dogs, who were barking up a storm. Hearing the commotion, the woman came to the doorway, pushed through the burlap hanging over the entrance, and called off the dogs. She advised me not to try to pet them, since they were half coyote and not really tame. Even she never tried to pet them; she just fed them. Turned out that she was a very pleasant conversationalist with a Christian Science background. Later, when I got home, Sandy had to take a picture of me, covered with dust, in my "Sunday-go-to-meetins" uniform. I dressed a little more casually for making farm calls from that point on.

To augment my modest salary, I set miles of fence posts, using a manual posthole digger in very rocky ground. Then I strung more miles of barbed wire to contain the wandering cattle. I honed my carpentry skills helping to build a house, then a hundred foot long hog parlor. I drove tractor – building my muscles by loading hundred pound sacks of wheat seed into the drill hoppers; and in doing all of that, I earned the respect of the farmers and ranchers in the community. (Fortunately, I never had to figure out how to milk a cow.) I don't begrudge all of those hours and days away from my study. My workday experiences gave me stories to illustrate the gospel to people in their familiar surroundings. Besides, this was nothing new to me. I'd been doing manual work to support the family since I started selling those newspapers down on the street corner when I was eight.

Satan's most effective tool for bringing down a Christian pastor is the temptation of pride. Most of us in this profession grew up having some sense of low self esteem. The role of pastor plays into that because that profession just naturally invites many compliments and praises from parishioners who want to express their appreciation for a good sermon, good Bible study, calling on a beloved parent when she/he was ill, or just being the "star attraction" at every worship service and church meeting. The problem is, if we pastors resonate with that praise, and we are not always vigilant to combat those damaging feelings, we'll start *"believing our own press."* We'll take too much credit for that in which we participated, in order to build up our self-esteem. When this occurs, the focus, in the pastor's mind, is on the pastor instead of on the Lord. Then, if we're not on our guard, that praise will become an addiction, causing us serious spiritual and mental injury, which can dramatically reduce our ability to accomplish the ministry to which we were called. Besides getting our marriage established on a solid foundation, this is reason number two why I needed to start my ministry in Hay.

This lifetime struggle with pride never goes completely away. The effectiveness of Satan's trickery is that he uses an item that is both good and necessary, which is praise and thanksgiving. But what ruins it is when the pastor begins to believe that he/she deserves it, and she/he begins to keep track of how many praises were given (how many "likes" on Facebook), as a measure of his/her worth and success as a person. So here is this young man who modestly envisioned himself as the glorious pastor of a two thousand-member church, straight out of graduate school, watching out for cow pies while making a pastoral call, then nailing together a hundred foot long hog parlor in the winter on windswept delta land next to the Snake River. When he hits his finger with the hammer, his fingers are so cold that he doesn't feel a thing—until later when he goes over to the fire barrel to warm up. Then his warming finger screams out in such pain he nearly wets his pants. *"Now,"* says the Lord, *"let's take a look at this reality of who you are and what you have to offer."*

Does that mean that I really didn't have much to offer to the Lord, in ministry? On the contrary. I had several important gifts and skills to use, quite effectively, for the kingdom work. When people have asked me what my spiritual gifts are, my response has always been: *"I have three spiritual gifts – Preaching, Teaching, and Administration."* But, until that pride of mine could be brought under control, my gifts would do more harm than good; because my pride would undo everything that my gifts accomplished. Over the years, I embraced more completely, the Apostle Paul's struggle with pride, found in 2 Corinthians 12:7ff. Paul struggled with what he called a thorn in his flesh. He prayed and prayed that this disabling intrusion into his life would be removed by God so that he could be at his best, his strongest and most virile, to serve the Lord with all his might. *"Lord, remove this from me so that I can do even greater things for Your kingdom . . ."*

"No," said the Lord God, *"I think I'll leave that thorn right where it is . . . My grace is sufficient for you, for My power is made perfect in weakness."* Paul's pride in his own skills would only get in the way of doing what the Lord God had in mind that needed to be done. At this point, Paul "got it." His real power, cleverness, skill set, does not get the job done that needs to be done. His willingness to meet God at his weakest point and let the grace of God fill him to accomplish God's will, and not his own, was his greatest privilege of all, in his service to the

kingdom. This too, was **an essential learning** for me. I am not present to use my skill set in ministry to accomplish my will in ministry, but to be available, to be a conduit, a vessel, a conveyor of the grace and healing power of the Lord to those who need to hear and receive what God has for them, that day. Of course, I don't know what those needs are, but God knows.

So here was coming to me, over time, **another learning** that would get my daily struggle with pride into alignment with God's grace. Working so hard on my sermons, of course, I want my hearers to catch my point, the moral to my story, the new understanding of God's love and activity in the world, which I have laid out in my sermon. Given that I have spent a good amount of time in writing that sermon, I see nothing wrong with that expectation, in itself. But where I can go wrong is when I discount the work of the Holy Spirit, who is using those same words, but tweaking their meaning /application to fit a particular person's need at this moment, which is quite different from the need of the person sitting across the aisle. In the economy of God, He can use those same words, that same phrase or train of thought, to meet the needs of a dozen folks with a variety of spiritual needs.

A good example of that happened after my retirement. I was scheduled to be the fill-in pastor for Labor Day weekend, while many church members and all the pastoral staff would be down at the coast for an annual church camping weekend in the Redwoods. I struggled for about two weeks with writing a sermon based upon the text, which reports Jesus' trial at Caiaphas' house. It particularly focused on Peter's betrayal of his Lord and his struggle with guilt. But why was I working on this theme? What's this got to do with the Gospel on Labor Day weekend? It's what I was compelled to write, but I could make no sense of it. After hours of mental struggles and debates with myself, I finished the sermon, still bewildered. Then came the Friday morning headlines in the newspaper that landed in my driveway. The beloved financial secretary for our church had been arrested and charged with embezzling $800,000 from the church, over a period of some years. Assuming her guilt, she'd be heading to prison for several years. So THAT was the reason for my sermon. But that was not the end. To use an old phrase, *"Not having a dog in this fight,"* I could be more objective about the issue, and not come under the microscope where people were looking to place blame in the heat of the moment. So with me preaching, not the regular staff, who were now under a cloud of "befuddlement" over how they could not have seen this, plus anger toward the woman, plus heartache, bewilderment and above all, the betrayal by a woman who was the dear and trusted friend of many, that engulfed the congregation, I was the right person to lead the congregation through this mess, on that Sunday morning. I took time in the middle of the service to *"address the elephant in the room."* After instructing them to make no judgment statements at this point – I gave the people the opportunity to share their initial feelings of shock, anger, bewilderment, despair, etc. That was cathartic. Then I preached the sermon, which turned out to be ideal for that moment in time.

At the close of the service, I marveled at the number of people who came up to me and told me how perfectly that sermon addressed their needs. Of course, I could not possibly have known those needs in advance. "They were all over the map." But what gave me a tremendous sense of holy appreciation that day was to see how God used me as a conduit of His healing, His comfort and His guidance during those critical moments. My great pleasure was not taken from some ill-conceived ego trip on how skillfully I'd handled an almost impossible situation. Rather, it derived from the sense of privilege I had of being able to participate with that Holy Presence as it moved among our people, responding to a wide range of needs. So now I am happy to receive compliments and praises for my efforts; but I keep no scorecard to bolster my ego. The genuine satisfaction comes in finding, in those kind words, that I have been open enough to the leading of the Spirit to be used by the Lord to accomplish His will in the lives of His beloved children.

8

Holiness in the Midst of the Commonplace

I GREW UP in the American Baptist "free church tradition." Being a part of the Free Church tradition we are not a liturgical people. We do not promote the sacraments, but rather, symbols (or ordinances) of spiritual realities. Ours is a "subjective" worship as opposed to the "objective" worship of the mass, as an example. In the objective church the salvation is in the physical object. So the water is blessed and becomes "holy water" which has within it the elements of salvation that are bestowed upon the candidate through baptism, whether or not that candidate is aware of what is happening to her/him. In the elements of the Eucharist, the bread is changed to the flesh and the wine is changed to the blood of Jesus and the transforming event is accomplished, whether any parishioner is spiritually involved or not. In the subjective church, the happening of the salvation event is subject to a human's spiritual involvement in what is taking place within him/her. The water is water. There are no salvation properties in it. It is symbolic of the grave only as we embrace that image in our hearts, making a conscious act of acceptance of the baptism as the drama describing the event of our death, burial and resurrection with the Christ, who went through the act of atonement on our behalf. We embrace His death as our death, His burial and His resurrection to *"newness of life"* as our resurrection (Romans 6:1-3). But no act of salvation has taken place if we have not been personally, spiritually and intellectually involved in embracing the experience. In the communion, the bread and juice/wine maintain their chemical compositions throughout the ceremony. They are symbols of what Christ did for us, just as they were symbols when Jesus held up the bread at the beginning of the meal, and the cup of wine at the end of the meal in the upper room of Mark's mother's home in Jerusalem. For the drama" to have value, we must be spiritually involved with the act for the "remembrance" with the contrition and deep sense of thankfulness for God's grace to have any spiritual value. It was an act done once and for all for us, not literally done again and again for us on a scheduled basis. We go through the drama, from time to time, not to accomplish the salvation act again and again, but to act as a reminder of the gracious, sacrificial act of love accomplished on our behalf, and an opportunity to be spiritually repaired and renewed in our faith as we move through that periodic "remembrance."

That being said, I have a deep respect for the sacred in worship. It developed when I was a teenager. For whatever reason that we youth would travel to other churches, on hot, summer Sunday nights, to attend evening worship services, we'd occasionally find ourselves in the presence of a preacher wearing his tee shirt in the pulpit. Given the heat, he'd start sweating, as he'd hold forth, and begin looking like he was in a "wet tee shirt contest;" except that what he was displaying was his hairy chest and hairy armpits. My youthful feelings ran way passed disgust, to feelings of sacrilege, and mockery of the holy things of God.

Then, years later, I was in graduate school in Berkeley, and a couple of us seminarians were to speak at First Baptist Church, Oakland, CA. So we sat up on the chancel. There was to be a baptism service for a couple of teenagers who had accepted Christ as their Savior. The associate pastor waded down into the baptistery wearing old cutoff jeans that were paint splattered, and again, a tee shirt that plastered itself to his unattractive torso. It took some self-control for me to contain my anger that he would treat this, one of the most sacred moments in these kids' spiritual lives, with so little dignity.

I have the same feeling about the pulpit. To me, the pulpit is not just a speaker's stand. It is the place where the congregation may rightfully expect to hear a Word from the Lord. I will offer up my intelligence, my life experiences, my own testimonies and/or the fruits of my prayerful guidance to proclaim, to the best of my ability and with the guidance of the Holy Spirit, a word of comfort, inspiration, admonition, instruction, or encouragement to those who have come to worship. I am most certainly a broken vessel seeking to be faithful; but I have confidence that God can use even my brokenness to convey His love to His people. I can ask no more. But in any event I cannot treat that pulpit lightly and with ignorance of what it represents.

Still, there are times when adjustments to respond to the present circumstances must reign. For example, though I embrace immersion as the most expressive mode of the salvation act, which we are expressing through baptism, there was the time when I would not immerse a young man because he had a fragile brain aneurism and was not supposed to have his head lower than his body. In that case, he stood in the baptistery, and I cupped water over his head. On another occasion, when I was chaplain at Children's Medical Center, the mother of a dying baby wanted me to baptize her newborn infant, before he died. It was not my belief in the need for infant baptism that led me to perform that ritual; rather, I was responding to the mother's grief and peace of mind, which moved me to gladly administer the baptism.

On another occasion, the hospital called me to come quickly; a patient wanted to be baptized before he died, and he had only a short time left. I grabbed my wife's sterling silver candy dish (which never got used for candy), and took it with me. I used it as my traveling baptismal font for years. I saw him lying on a gurney, with an oxygen mask and wires and tubes hooked up to him. I asked him the necessary questions, but could not understand his responses. So I removed his oxygen mask to hear better. His lips quickly turned blue. So I put the mask back in place and continued assuming that he was giving the appropriate replies, then baptized him. He immediately relaxed and expressed what gratefulness he could muster. A couple of months later he contacted me and asked me to officiate at his wedding. He obviously had made a remarkable recovery. He lived a happy life with his bride and then died of cancer, five years later.

Some liturgical events are just plain funny, no matter how serious the worshipful occasion. One January, during Pocatello's coldest subzero days, a woman and I scheduled her baptism for an agreed upon Sunday, when the husband's favorite football team would not be playing. On Saturday the custodian remembered that he had not filled the baptistery. He ran down to turn on the water and flip the switch for the submersible heater unit. The only problem was, without thinking, he flipped on the switch for the submersible heating element before he started the water, which, unbeknownst to us, burned out the element. The January frigid air penetrated the high brick wall and came cascading down into the baptistery area, almost like a wind. When I tested the water, it was so cold, it stung my fingers.

I called the woman and suggested that we postpone the baptism for a week. *"Absolutely not,"* she said, *"I talked my husband into coming to the service this week; he sure will not come on another Sunday."*

So I instructed her, *"Okay, you wait at the top of the steps until I have said all of the words I need to say. Then you come down the stairs and don't stop for anything, just keep coming."* Well, she did. The look on her face nearly cracked me up when her foot hit the water. As she descended the stairs she started sucking air. By the time the water got to her sensitive areas, she nearly squealed, but kept control. I loved her for her determination. She was well baptized. But I had a hard time keeping a straight face.

On one occasion in Salt Lake City, a 30ish age man accepted Christ and wanted to unite with the First Baptist Church, but he wanted me to baptize him in the creek that runs through the Baptist camp up in the Wasatch Mountains above North Ogden. The creek flowed rapidly through the camp in that area, and it was not deep enough for a stand-up baptism. So I got on my knees amongst those river rocks and he sat down. All went well until I leaned him back under the water, at which point his body started to float in those rapids. I'm proud to say that I was strong enough to hang onto his shirt, as he started heading downstream, and pull him back to where he could get his footings. That was another thoroughly baptized Christian. We had a good laugh when we both got back on shore. In some of the most serious moments, it's wonderful to be able to laugh once in awhile. Even God has a great, if occasionally annoying, sense of humor.

On a couple of Holy Land tours, members of the tour group asked me to baptize them in the Jordan River. For some, it was a re-baptism, for others, a first time baptism. In an area of the river, just south of the Galilean Lake, there is enough water for baptisms in a well-groomed area that includes a concrete ramp and railing down into the river. It works well. But what I would see, while standing there, which others would not necessarily see, through the murky water, were huge suckers swimming quietly and sleekly around and through our legs – but never touching us. I found it interesting to be baptizing people in the midst of fish the size of salmon; but I was thankful that some of my squeamish candidates did not look down to see what was swimming around their feet and legs.

9

Expanding Influence and a Painful Lesson About Submission

AMONG THE BENEFITS that came my way, while being in Hay, were the opportunities to be a representative to the various judicatory bodies of the denomination. Representing small churches in sparsely populated areas, gave me the privilege of serving on a variety of denominational positions which allowed me a broader view of denominational ministry and structure, and gave me the opportunity to meet many influential and knowledgeable leaders that I'd never have had the chance to meet, in the much more competitive atmosphere of the city settings. In Hay, I found myself, over time, in a number of positions at the regional level of the denomination, participating in the decision to re-design the shape of our administrative unit for better, more efficient use of our resources and support groups. Years later, these connections ultimately led me to develop friendships with three different folks who served as General Secretary of the denomination, while I served in positions on the General Board, which put me in the position to be called up to the Executive

Committee of the General Board of the American Baptist Churches, USA, which was the highest elective position one could hold. At that level, I was able to help redesign some of our overall youth ministry goals and programmatic guidelines for youth, which came out in a book authored by Jeffrey Jones entitled, *Youth Ministry: Making and Shaping Disciples.* I also had influence in reshaping our relationship to the National Council of Churches, USA, plus, helping to reshape that Council itself, in how it relates its ministries to the various supporting denominations. Some of that work was accomplished with and through Dr. Jitsuo Morikawa, a denominational leader whom I had admired from afar, since I was a youth. The fact that he embraced me as fully as he did, and offered me his friendship, has given me a personal sense of pride for years

In the meantime, as I developed my craft as a pastor in Hay, I started trying to be creative in my pastoral programs that reached out beyond my Sunday morning sermon, Sunday school classes, and midweek Bible study. There were several folks in that congregation, whom we admired, and from whom we found friendship and support. To mention just a couple, there was Maryette Camp, our church organist and mother of two children, one on each side of six years of age. She was a farm wife who became a good friend to Sandy. Her grandfather was Chris Bennett. He and his wife were immigrants from England. He was a "gentleman farmer" – well dressed even in his bib overalls, intellectual, and a deeply devoted Christian. His wife was badly crippled, but showed inspiring tenacity in putting on a pair of Chris' bib overalls, then going out to lay down on her stomach, and with her elbows, pull herself through her garden, as she weeded and pruned her plants.

I got into the mode of trying some city style ministries. With a couple, I hoped to engage the larger community in events outside of the local church. The others were attempted offerings to the congregation to experience the Christian life and ministry in different ways than they were used to. They each, in turn, fell flat. All of this perceived rejection finally earned me a trip to the hospital, where I was introduced to a drug called Valium, to calm me down to the point where I could function again.

Failing again and again to develop the ministries that I believed I should be doing, I decided it was time to move on to another church. I had my name circulated around the country. I don't know how many churches looked at my name, but I know that at least nine Pastoral Search Committees turned me down. So I applied for a camp director's position in California. It was pretty much a matter of *"I'll do anything to get out of Hay."* I was accepted for an interview, and made my plane reservations.

God has spoken to me several times through Sandy. The first time happened at the lunch table when she said, casually, *"It'll sure seem strange to just be a regular part of the congregation again."* She didn't know the importance of her remark; but it hit me smack between the eyes. *"That's right! I'm not meant to be a regular part of the congregation. God called me into pastoral ministry and He has not called me out of pastoral ministry."*

When lunch was over, I went to my study and prayed, *"Lord, I will stay in Hay for the rest of my life and serve You here in whatever way I can, if that is Your will for me."* At that moment I meant every word of what I prayed. I called and cancelled my job interview, and then

I cancelled my plane reservations. Within an hour, I got a call about two church openings: One in central Washington, and one in Seattle. I chose the church in central Washington, and I was directed to the church in Seattle. Very soon, we were on our way to the Columbia Baptist Church in the Columbia City neighborhood of south Seattle. God needed my self-surrender and my submission to His will before He could do anything with me to help me fulfill my calling for ministry in His kingdom on earth. When it finally came, we could move on.

10

From Wheat and Cattle to the City

A PATTERN THAT DEVELOPED through the years of my ministry was that every place I said that I would never go is precisely where I accepted a call. In school, I had said that I was a city boy; I could never pastor a rural church. (You remember what I said about that cow.) And so, what was the first church out of school that I agreed to pastor? Yep. Hay, Washington. It turned out to be a lifesaver, and essential to my future ministries. It gave Sandy and me time to get to know each other, to fashion our marriage into a God-ordaining union, and to build our relationship on a solid foundation of life and ministry together. The second, absolutely essential thing it gave me, was a chance to get over myself, so that God could do what He needed to do with me to make me effective in ministry in His Kingdom.

Again, as you recall, when I was finally ready to move on in ministry, I was given a choice of two churches to explore. I told my Executive Minister that by now, I'm familiar with eastern Washington culture and life issues; I'll take the offer to explore ministry from the central Washington church. So of course, I became pastor of the Seattle church. Little did I know that I would now begin my ministry to troubled churches.

When we accepted the call to the Seattle church, we met some wonderful people, and were introduced to the world of Boeing Aircraft culture. During those glory days of Boeing, their employment rose to 102,000 employees, strung out from Renton, Washington, north to Everett. Then came the Boeing crash. The employment of Boeing workers dropped from 102,000, to 38,000, in eighteen months. When that buying power evaporated almost overnight, all manner of support businesses closed their doors. Auto dealerships closed, furniture stores shut down. Upscale homes on both sides of Lake Washington, went into foreclosure, with lending institutions taking out ads in the newspapers, begging people not to just move out of their homes. *"Please, come in. Let us help you work something out."* (The lending institutions didn't want those houses sitting vacant and becoming targets for vandals and thieves.) Chemists and engineers with advanced degrees and educational awards found themselves trying to get onto the welfare rolls for which they were not eligible. The suicide rate went up, and the psychiatrists' couches filled up. Our church folks joined those who were driving to Central Washington to get gleaned potatoes to bring back to the Seattle area, both to distribute to the hungry, and to prepare meals to feed hungry people who were sitting in their unheated, unlit homes. It got so bad that someone paid for a billboard sign out near SeaTac, International Airport that read, *"Will the last person out of Seattle please turn out the lights."*

There were a number of noteworthy folks in this congregation. I'll mention only a few who are representative of several especially good folks. Darlene Dahlgren took over as church organist after Mutso Homma retired. Darlene was also the woman who took care of all of the older women in the church, giving them rides to circle meetings, caring about some physical needs, getting them to their Bible studies. She seemed indispensible. But she also looked forward to the day when her reclusive husband would retire from his job. She wanted to travel. They had enough money they could afford it. She had sat at home for much of his employment years and now she was ready to head out and see the world. But he had different plans. When he retired, he came home, sat down in a chair in front of the television set and announced that that was where he intended to stay. That broke Darlene's heart and her spirit. Within a few months, she succumbed to liver cancer. Near the end, she was so jaundiced that I could barely tell her apart from the yellow hospital blanket covering her bed. What a peculiar position I found myself in. I told her that the congregation was holding a prayer meeting, in about an hour, for her recovery. But Darlene wanted to die. She didn't want that prayer meeting. She wanted me to pray to God that He would take her home. Her choice was to remain on earth and be condemned to existing with that uncommunicative husband at home, or go into that glorious eternal life in heaven for which we all yearn. *"If heaven is so beautiful, why would you want me to stay here in this dismal place?"* she asked me. I had no answer for that; so I prayed that God's will would be done.

From Darlene's hospital bed, I went to the church to the called prayer meeting to pray for God's divine intervention to heal Darlene. I told the congregation that Darlene wanted to die. That was totally unacceptable to the congregation. Who will play the organ? More importantly, who will take care of the old ladies? So here we were: praying for God's will to be life and healing, while Darlene was praying for God's will to be death. In the end, Darlene's wishes were fulfilled. She died within a week. She died of a broken heart, which had made her defenseless against her disease. Meanwhile, I had to have God's help in getting me passed some huge resentment issues against her husband as I prepared her funeral service.

Jim Telgenhoff was also a remarkable person. An electrician and skilled laborer, he stepped up and helped out in so many ways, while giving board leadership in the church. He and his wife Shirley became our personal friends for decades. We visited and camped together. Edna Schmalbeck was another special person – a schoolteacher, who could work wonders with the children in the church, and so it went. Oh yes! There was Irene Owens. Irene Owens was a Black nurse at Haborview Hospital. She worked around the church in so many different areas, helping here and there. I was proud of our congregation the day I overheard a half dozen women talking together, about Irene. One person in the group didn't know her. Others tried to describe her. She's a nurse up at Harborview. She works in the women's group, she does a lot of work with our youth. She's always out here in the Narthex on Sunday mornings greeting people. It never crossed anyone's mind to say, "*She's the Black lady who works with our kids.*" I felt like, "*We've arrived!*"

One of the **great life lessons** that I've received through the years came from Reuben Triebwasser, a rough-around-the-edges steel worker, and remarkable human being, who gave me a valuable new insight. One day, he and I were standing out on the street curb on south Edmunds, in front of our old Columbia church home, working on some small project. Seemingly out of the blue, he said, "*I haven't smoked a cigarette in thirteen years.*"

I responded, "*You gave up smoking, thirteen years ago?*"

"*Oh, no,*" he said. "*I haven't given up smoking. The day I give up smoking I'll go right back to it. I have a half a pack of unsmoked cigarettes in my top drawer. No, I just choose not to smoke, today. And I've been choosing not to smoke today for thirteen years.*"

I have used this illustration countless times in counseling sessions and private conversations. I've used it to control my own harmful inclinations. We're all addicted to something, and tempted to some other things. We can't give anything up forever. But we can choose not to do it today, or in the next hour. And then we can make the same choice later today, or tomorrow, as many times as is necessary. That **life lesson** was a priceless gift to me, and for many others, with whom I've shared it.

This was the era of the racial revolution and the racial riots taking place across the nation. Watts burned in 1965. Detroit burned down about a year later. Other cities experienced racial upheavals, including Seattle. I belonged to a Black Clergy Ministerial Assn. Several of my friends had taped compact mirrors to walking canes, so they could look for bombs under their vehicles, before they got into their cars. Being part of that group, I became compromised in the eyes of some. I learned never to sit with my back to an open-curtained window. It became a practice I needed to observe for the remainder of my years as a pastor. I got used to seeing unmarked police cars parked in the dark of night around my neighborhood.

Our congregation was multi-racial. The majority was from European ancestry. We also had folks who were of Chinese, Japanese, Filipino, and African ancestry. We got along with total equality within the walls of the church. But our youth, representing a variety of racial backgrounds, had to deal with the reality of racial divisions in their high schools. White students had to try to remain safe by staying out of "Black hallways" while Black students had to be wary of "White hallways" at Franklin High. At one point, racial tensions ran so high at Rainier Beach High School that the principal was barricaded into his office and the National Guard had to be brought in to restore and maintain order. For a while, I had to escort our Japanese American foster daughter through the halls of Rainier Beach High School, for her safety. Some of our African American church members were disparaged by their Black acquaintances for worshipping in a predominately White church. Some of the Japanese American folks were labeled with the derogatory name of "*Banana*" ("*Yellow on the outside, White on the inside*") by the Japanese ancestry community for associating with, and worshipping with White Americans. In fact, one of our Japanese Baptist Church pastors was fired for talking with me about some joint ministries, together. (He was already suspect in the eyes of the congregation, since he was of Japanese ancestry while his wife was of European ancestry.) Maintaining a quality, healing, and witnessing ministry, while continuing to declare the equality of all people through Jesus Christ in the midst of racial diversity, requires patience, perseverance, prayer, ingenuity, and a whole lot of Christian grace, during periods of racial hatred and resentment.

On the block where our home was, there were people with Jewish, Filipino, Chinese, African, and European, ancestries. Our five-year-old daughter could go across the street and play with Teresa, who was Black. She could go next door and play with Doris and Carol, who were Chinese. But she couldn't figure out why she could not bring Teresa over, with her, to play at Doris and Carol's house. We could not adequately explain racial discrimination between groups without prejudicing her mind. So we gave her some non-committal response that almost certainly was not helpful.

Not only was the racial revolution fully underway, the Hippie Revolution was also in full swing. These folks were wearing colorful, outlandish clothes, railing against Capitalism and the "Military-Industrial Complex." They also replaced the "Swing And Sway With Sammy Kaye" music, along with Glenn Miller and Artie Shaw, with folk music. The Ink Spots were replaced by the Everly Brothers; Frank Sinatra was replaced by Bob Dylan, while Janis Joplin replaced Rosemary Clooney. Folk music was not about love and romantic moments between a man and a woman; it was about social injustice, the devastations of war, and putting an end to the traditional social structures and courtesies of what had been the common guidelines for living in community.

Not surprisingly, this movement dramatically impacted my church youth group. Since we had some creative kids among our youth, I decided to see if I could get out ahead of the curve, and lead them from the front, rather than prodding them from the rear. This got a bit tricky since Baptists have traditionally taken a stand against social dancing. (That was not my personal position. I absolutely loved social dancing from about 8ᵗʰ grade, on. I mourned the thought that once I was ordained, I'd have to give up my dancing.) I decided that our youth group should organize, and host, a Hootenanny in our church fellowship hall, inviting all of the other American Baptist youth groups in the Puget Sound area. We got the folk song artists lined up, and the response to that invitation was far greater than we ever expected. The music was engaging, everyone was standing because we were jammed in, wall to wall; and happy feet cannot keep from dancing. Because the music was so loud, I took pity on the neighbors and kept the windows and doors closed, on a very hot (for Seattle) evening. Soon, we were all sweating with our hair plastered to our heads, and one girl after another grabbed me to dance with her – their pastor was DANCING!!! We had a fabulous time. Then, of course, those youth went back to their home churches and wanted to do the same thing in their places of worship. That's when the angry calls started coming my way from youth leaders and pastors up and down the Puget Sound area. I didn't care; it was a great event; and it sure didn't hurt my reputation with the kids.

Two major issues confronted me, apart from normal pastoral activities. The first issue was concerned with the brokenness in the congregation. My predecessor had to share an office with the church secretary. Over a period of time, they developed a friendship, by the very nature of the job and a lack of privacy for each of them. It had never become sexual, nor did either of them want that. But one day, in a moment of exuberance about something that had happened in the church, he kissed her. He was immediately remorseful – overcome with guilt. He went to the husband and apologized to him, then he went home to his wife, told her what had happened, and asked her for forgiveness. Forgiveness was not forthcoming. In more recent times we'd say that this pastor's wife *"went ballistic!"* She went around the church accusing this *"vixen"* of seducing her husband. The pastor's wife wanted her expelled from the congregation. This forced the congregation to choose sides. It got bad enough that the denominational Executive Minister came to the pastor and told him that he wasn't going to weather this issue, and he should quickly move on. There was a missionary church in another state that would accept him. They left, and Sandy and I arrived, not knowing about this *"little bump in the road."*

It was not long before members of the congregation started getting letters from that pastor's wife asking them how they could stand to attend worship with that *"whore of Babylon"* singing in the choir loft. Her presence was contaminating the whole service. Other letters of a similar nature came to me. Members of the congregation started asking me questions like, *"If a pastor can't control himself against sin, what chance have I got of avoiding a fall?" "If a pastor's wife can't find forgiveness in her heart, what chance have I got of forgiving those who have wronged me?" "If the Christian Faith can't help them past their problems, what good is it to me?"* I had to spend a significant amount of time on a personal learning curve discovering how to identify, and deal with, the consequences of sin committed by spiritual leaders. I invested a fair amount of time with individuals, and the congregation, trying to keep the faith community from tearing itself apart, and to keep them a gracious and loving community, which, by the grace of God, we succeeded in doing.

I learned to get the church folks to convert their feelings of anger, suspicion, and resentment to feelings of genuine pity over human sin and that pastor's wife's mental distress. Then, in time, the emotion of pity could be more easily let go, and the congregation moved on. However, this damage done to a congregation gave me the first taste of the kind of collateral damage that a pastor's sin can perpetrate, far beyond the event itself.

The second issue was that the church had plans to enter a major building project, before I was employed as their pastor. Initially, the plan was to purchase the property next door, tear down the house on that lot, and add a Christian Education wing to the main body of the church building. We offered the woman who owned the home the market value of her house plus ten percent, plus, we'd move her to a place of her choosing anywhere in the greater Seattle area. She was interested in moving out of that neighborhood; so it was going to be a done deal, until her boyfriend got greedy and talked her into really jacking up the price on the premise that we needed that property so badly that we'd pay anything to get it. Sadly for her, she listened to him.

It was at this point that I was about to gain **a crucial learning** about how I saw myself. When our neighbor made her choice, we had to make ours: We withdrew our original offer and ended our attempt to buy her property. Taking a work break, one morning, I walked around the neighborhood. Down at the other end of the block were three old, uninhabited houses that needed to be torn down. I thought to myself: Why not sell our present church building, buy those lots, and start from scratch to build a new church home, that can be expanded later, as the congregation grows? We'll have much more space, modern, multi-purpose rooms, a parking lot, and . . . we'll be directly across the street from the Northwest School For The Blind, where I'd hoped we could have a ministry anyway? My growing excitement was infectious, and many members of the congregation got on board. Other folks began to spin their own dreams of what we might accomplish in a brand new church home.

We did a lot of preparatory work on what we'd have to accomplish to achieve our dream. Then, we called a business meeting to ask for the congregation's support to begin the process of selling and buying property to accomplish our ministries of the present and future. A good share of the congregation members present were on board, ready to vote in favor of the project. Then, Les Hall took the floor. Les was a devoted Christian. He also was the quintessential old curmudgeon financial guy who kept our books. I picture him hunched over his roll top desk with sharpened pencils in a cup, wearing a green visor eyeshade, perusing a spreadsheet. He said, *"We can't afford it."* The numbers don't add up. Congregation members argued with him. *"Nope." "Won't work." "The money's not there,"* were his responses again and again.

Then I noticed a change of tone in the meeting. Members were starting to make personal attacks on Lester. The comments were moving away from the immediate subject at hand to personal attacks on the individual. Suddenly, I was at a moment of truth. It came in the format of a question I had to ask about myself: *"Am I the CEO/Business Manager of a Christian corporation, or am I the pastor of a congregation?"* If I'm the Business Manager, then I want my corporation to achieve its goals of growth in size and services to the community, whatever it takes. If I am, first of all, the pastor of a congregation, then I'm the pastor, the shepherd, of all the people, regardless of their positions on any given issue. In this case, I was Lester's pastor, as well as the pastor of those who were supporting my – and their – dream. I went up front and stood with Les. I praised him for his deeply held concern; I acknowledged his financial expertise, and his dedication to our church community. Then I suggested that we step away from the matter before us, until we have studied all the issues, addressed all of the financial challenges, and projected our future resources, before we come together again. I was standing against my own personal goals in order to protect a member of my flock who was under attack. I thank God that this **crucial learning** about the heart of my ministry came to me early in my profession.

Later, we did sell our church building to the Boy's Club, and went down to the other end of the block where we bought three properties, tore down the houses, and prepared to build the first stage of a new church home complex, leaving the woman next door to deal with all those boys who started coming to the Boys' Club. (Sadly for her, she soon had to sell out at a much-reduced price.)

Thanks to our church finance guy, Les Hall, we knew that we could not financially afford to build a whole new complex unless we acted as our own general contractor, and constructed most of it ourselves. People said, *"That's okay. We can do that; because we hired our new pastor as a building pastor, anyway."*

They did what?! I'm only twenty-eight years old! What were they thinking! But as I got to reflecting on it, I'd had plenty of training in carpentry, painting, electrical and plumbing from my days as a maintenance guy at the school, while working through my graduate program. And what had I been doing for nearly three years in Hay? Construction. I knew how to talk the talk. I could tell when a sub-contractor was trying to jerk me around; and I sure knew how to swing a hammer, build concrete forms, and run power saws. I also had to negotiate loans and raise the money to pay them off, and encourage volunteers to show up at the work site. I guess I was the building pastor, after all. Beyond that, Bill Cox, a Christian contractor with excellent people skills, and a contractor's license, stepped up and gave us directions from the blueprints, and had the ability to organize volunteers into the most effective work teams to accomplish the various projects. I also admired Bill's people skills. He could move a guy off a chop saw, who was ruining valuable lumber, and demote him to sweeping floors, and make the fellow feel good about the new opportunity he was given.

I got to lead our congregation in ministry in our new church home for about two years. One day, I got a letter in the mail from my good friend and fellow pastor, Bob Brattstrom. He said that he'd been reading my weekly church newsletters, and he could tell from my writings that it was time for me to move on. His challenge got me to realizing that I had used up all of my clout in getting that building constructed. I was in a comfortable, fur-lined rut, since most of the people in the congregation really liked and supported me. But I could no longer motivate the people to do ministry in their new church home. When I reflected on his observations, I realized

Bob was right. After all the work we had done to get that new church home, I wanted to hang around and enjoy it for a few years; but I knew in my heart of hearts, that was not to be. So before long, we'd be heading out of town to a new ministry. (THEN!! That dirty rat Bob, became a candidate for Columbia, and took my old job as pastor! Fine thing! Well, I'm glad he could do it – but I gave him a bad time over that for a while, just for orneriness' sake.)

Edna Schmalbeck, whom I mentioned above, upon learning of my resignation as pastor, wrote this letter to Sandy and me:

Dear George and Sandy,

When Wiggie called us in Reading and told us of your leaving Columbia, we were left with a state of disbelief. We lay awake that night and discussed it until early morning but came up with nothing relevant to understanding.

We have appreciated and valued your service to our congregation for the past six years. Columbia has never had a more capable, intelligent and loving leadership in the 25 years we have been members.

George, your sermons are the best we have ever heard. Each one is a scholarly masterpiece that stirs our thinking and our conscience. You have served in our church and communicate in areas far beyond any expectations. Your clear-sighted vision has made us believe we are capable of greater things. Your constant faith in the growth of our church and that we would be able to surmount our financial crisis has never seemed daunting. You have never evidenced discouragement. This has been a source of strength for us all.

Sandy, you are an inspiration to everyone. Your sweet, quiet humility does not hide your beautiful talent of which you have given so generously in every area of service, including teaching, music, leadership and your exemplary family life. When you extended your love to mother another girl we just felt, "That's just what Sandy would do!"

You have both been so kind in helping our family in times of need and in sustaining our faith when we needed strength. We shall ever be grateful for the help you gave Mona and I during that 17-hour vigil three years ago when Lee had heart surgery.

Our deep regret at your leaving must be selfishness on our part. We would like to keep you forever. Lee and I feel that your missions with us are not complete.

We are filled with remorse at ourselves that we haven't worked harder in our church to have made your burdens lighter.

I do believe that a bit of each one of us dies when one we love and rely upon so much leaves.

You will ever be in our prayers.

May God love you, bless you and prosper you in your new work.

We shall always love you.

Lee and Edna Schmalbeck.

11

Did I Say I'd Never Go To . . . ?

THE ANNUAL GATHERING of our American Baptist Region of the Northwest was held in Boise, Idaho, in 1971. During a break, my friend and I headed to a restaurant for lunch. We were barred at the door from entering because my friend was Black. I was shocked beyond words, at that late date in our history, that such overt racism would be so glaringly displayed. As we walked away, I swore I'd never take a church in Idaho. So naturally, two weeks later, I received a letter from the Pulpit Committee of First Baptist Church, Pocatello, Idaho.

As we researched information about the city and the church, we learned that Pocatello, with a population, at that time, of 40,000, had 42 Mormon Ward Houses (congregations). I remembered back to graduate school where the prevailing wisdom was not to serve in a Mormon community while our children were at an impressionable age. At age three and six, our kids certainly qualified for being at an "impressionable age;" but Sandy and I doubted that the Mormon culture could be any more threatening to our children than the secular, crime-ridden, drug-saturated culture of Seattle.

It didn't take me long to discover that I had become the pastor of a congregation that was in danger of splitting. And worse: My secretary was one of the ringleaders in the mischief. Before I arrived on the scene, the young adults, who represented about forty church members, had been in conversations with a young adult group from the First Congregational Church, a couple of blocks away. Their plan was to join forces. Together, they would take over the First Baptist Church building, which was much newer and offered more varieties of rooms, and give the older generation in both churches, the Congregational Church bldg., which was much older, far more limited in space, and with many typical problems of an aging building. My secretary, who highly resented me for accepting the call and replacing her beloved former pastor, who'd moved on for his own reasons, was heavily involved in the secret negotiations. In an effort to make me ineffective, she sabotaged some of my work. It was a time when secretaries still took dictation and typed correspondence to be sent out. When I learned that she was changing some of the key words in my correspondence and directives to make me look bad, or cause the opposite to happen than I intended, I had to fire her; and the whole scheme of the young adults in their Sunday school class began to unravel. In short order, that entire class, who represented most of the young families in the church, left our congregation. Only then could we begin to build a ministry, which the people, twenty years later, looked back upon as "the golden years."

One of the things that's very hard to do as a pastor, is to develop personal friendships among the people he/she is serving. I could not develop personal friendships in Hay; but when we moved to Seattle, people from Hay would drop in to see us, to visit, and to enjoy our company. In Seattle, I could not develop personal friendships; but once we moved to Pocatello, several people, one family in particular, became fast friends and visited us, and camped with us, once we moved to Pocatello. One of the dilemmas for the pastor is that if I'm able to develop personal friendships with these folks, those folks will become jealous that I don't spend personal time with them. So I followed the pattern, I was friendly with many, but had no personal friendships in Pocatello. There was one exception to that: I'll call him Richard.

Richard was a very engaging, handsome young man in his late 30's. His wife and younger daughter were quite active in the church. He wanted nothing to do with the church, or God. His goal was to become a millionaire by the time he was 40. He worked for his father-in-law in a glass and paint store. His father-in-law had no more use for God and church than Richard had. Richard liked his women. When the traveling salesmen came through, they usually had a woman or two that would take them on in a motel room, and Richard regularly joined the party. He also had become an alcoholic. One day, it all caught up with him. He got into his Cadillac and drove a couple of hundred miles to another city with the intention of committing suicide. He rented a motel room to spend the night. In the morning, he'd drive up to the top of a bluff overlooking the city, and drive off the bluff.

In the morning, as he was getting ready to leave, it crossed his mind that he might discover, on the other side, that there is a God there, after all. So just in case, maybe he ought to introduce himself. So he got down on his knees next to the bed and prayed, "*God, if you are there, I'm sorry I'm doing this."*

"Then why are you doing it?!" The voice was clear and loud. Richard looked around the room and saw no one. So he prayed again: *"God, I'm sorry for what I'm about to do."*

"Then why are you doing it?!" The voice was just as loud and just as confronting as before.

"I don't know," he said. So Richard got up and looked around the room. There on the bed stand was an open Gideon Bible, which he had not noticed, before. I no longer remember the verse that his eyes fell upon, but it was precisely what he needed to read. He called his wife and told her that he was heading home. He'd tell her all about it when he saw her. She called me, greatly relieved.

He saw me the next day. He related to me his encounter with God. Then he accepted Christ as his Savior, and we set up his baptism for a week later. Now came a string of wonders. First of all, his father-in-law fired him. He didn't want any Christians working for him.

Richard was the breadwinner of the family; so what was he to do? He decided to open his own store, though he didn't have any money. His plan was to develop a picture framing shop that would include a Christian bookstore in one part of the store. Just a block away from the church sat a storefront bldg. that had been vacant for a couple of years. The landlord was grateful to have someone in the building, so he accepted the rental agreement on a handshake. Richard got the place cleaned out and then said that he needed some glass cases and countertops. An old business friend said that he knew a man who owned a warehouse, who had a bunch of display cases taking up space in that warehouse, and the owner wanted to get rid of them. So now, he had his glass cases. Next, he decided that he needed a cash register that records sales. Just as he had prayed about glass cases, so now, he prayed about what he should do in regards to a cash register. As he drove along the residential portion of North Arthur, one day, a voice said to him, *"Stop here and go up to that house."* He thought that was weird; but what, in his life, wasn't weird these days? So he went up the porch steps to the door, rang the bell, and said to the man who opened the door, *"I don't know what I am doing here, but I need a cash register."*

The homeowner said, *"I repair cash registers and I have a basement full of them. Let's go see what we can find."* Richard found what he needed and the man said, *"I can make you a very good deal on it."* In the meantime, during all the weeks that it took to get established and up and running, once a week, an anonymous envelope with $200 was slipped under the store door. Once the store was opened for business, the envelopes stopped coming. Richard never discovered who his benefactor was; but that amount of money had much more buying power in those days than today, and was essential for putting food on the table and paying necessary bills. Several unframed pictures and memorabilia pieces that Sandy and I had in the back of our closets were given to him to frame, which he then hung around the store as examples of possibilities that hopefully would catch the eye of potential customers once his store was open.

All during this time, since Richard had lost all of his old friends, and because he was a very social guy, he'd show up at my office every weekday morning at 10 a.m., and we'd head down to the bowling alley for coffee and a roll. We talked about a lot of things Christian, about his work experience and past life. Above all, we became fast friends. He was the first deeply personal friend I'd ever had in ministry. At the same time, he got immersed in church life. Then, one day, an issue arose. I have no idea what it was; but I had to "pull rank" on him and be his confronting pastor rather than his supportive friend. He walked away and never came for another coffee date. He continued his ministries. I had told a Gideon about his motel Bible experience. The Gideons approached Richard and he became a regular speaker for them. Eventually, they settled in another church, and our family moved to Salt Lake City. His store thrived. But I decided that it was too painful to try to be both a pastor and personal friend to my parishioners. It took a lot of years and a lot of miles, all the way to Medford, Oregon, for me to get passed that pain.

Still, I must honor him as a remarkable man. Others in that Pocatello church that I might highlight, would be Barbara and Dwight Mitchem. Dwight was manager of the Penny's Department Store across the street from the church. Barbara was a deeply devoted Christian and a remarkable study leader among the women. One thing she taught the women was "conversational prayer." The concept is based upon the scriptural statement that *"Where two or three are gathered together in my name, there am I, in their midst"* (Matt. 18:20, RSV). So Jesus being part of the group, as discussion goes along they would address one another, and address Jesus with a question, a need for guidance, a concern for a neighbor, etc., just as you would engage any other participant in the group.

Four to five years into my ministry in Pocatello, I challenged our folks in a way that I've not heard has been done elsewhere. The Columbia folks in Seattle had fallen into a malaise in their congregational life. When I was pastor there, undertaking the new church home building project, we secured a loan from the denomination that included a balloon payment in ten years. The ten years was upon them, and they didn't have the $20,000, to make that mortgage payment. Sandy and I had been in Seattle, and learned of their plight. On our way home to Pocatello, I began working on a plan. I challenged the Pocatello church to formally offer the Seattle church a dollar match challenge, up to $10,000. We supported mission projects, from time to time. This was a mission project. The only difference was, it was not an overseas congregation, it was a church community in Seattle. I knew that our congregation could come up with that much money without breaking a sweat. The greater question appeared to be whether or not the Seattle people could come up with their $10,000. Well, our apparent "faith" in them, and our generous offer, took hold in their struggling congregation. Those folks came to life. One waitress pledged all of her tips. An older person cashed in her extensive coin collection. Some young people pledged their baby-sitting money; and so it went. Their money started rising on their side of the thermometer on the wall.

Now, the Pocatello people had to get busy; but our matching funds were slow in matching their dollars. In fact, it began to look like we might not meet our end of the bargain. What was the matter? Then I found out that the moneyed people in our congregation decided to step back and see if George could pull this off on his own. They couldn't see any reason to underwrite any portion of their pastor's "pet project." So it became a real challenge for me to get the less moneyed folks to join me in holding up our end of the bargain. I shared with our congregation, the stories they were sending to me of the self-sacrifices being made by the folks in that congregation. That spurred most of us to a greater response. In the end, we matched the funds and they got their $20,000. I made sure that we had a great celebration, and read their many thank you letters. Then, Jim and Shirley Telgenhoff traveled to Pocatello, to thank us from the pulpit, for one sister church helping another sister church get over the hump. He also wanted us to know that we'd rejuvenated the congregation to do ministry. All the moneyed folks ever said to me, from the sidelines, was, "*I didn't think you could do it.*"

12

Learning the Dynamics
of the Mormon Culture

EVERY GENTILE, (any non-Mormon, including Jews, who lives in a predominately Mormon community), has to come to grips with how he/she shall survive the dominant culture. It is a culture that permeates every part of the day from the clock radio coming on in the morning to the television going off in the evening. It affects business, employment, career promotions, housing sales and rentals, politics, social issues – even holidays, where Pioneer Day, on July 24th, (celebrating when Brigham Young and his followers entered the Salt Lake Valley and he declared, *"This is the place"*), is a bigger celebration than Independence Day on July 4th. In the Salt Lake Valley, in Utah, even the street addresses are based upon the location of the Mormon Temple. Our home address in Salt Lake City was 715 South 1100 East. That means our home was located seven blocks south of the temple and eleven blocks east of the temple.

The Church of Jesus Christ of Latter Day Saints has a profound influence in the social dynamics of life in the public schools. As in Utah, so in southeast Idaho, every high school has an L.D.S. seminary nearby. That is a place for Mormon religious instruction to be incorporated into the local high school as a complimentary contribution to the public school curricula. The school bell that rings in the high school will also ring in the seminary across the street. In signing up students for public school classes, the counselors will typically sign up all students for seminary classes, as well, unless the student says "No." One of the ways that students, not part of the Mormon majority, could be socially isolated, was that in the seminary, the announcement might be made, for example, that Friday is dress-up day. All the girls will be wearing dresses; all the boys will be wearing suits or nice sweaters/ties, in contrast to the casual dress that is typical. So on Friday, the Gentile kids (who *didn't get the memo*") show up in their standard "grungies" while the Mormon kids are all decked out, leaving the Gentile kids to miss out on the dress code of the day – which is a very important issue for teenagers, particularly when they are a minority to begin with.

Years later, when we moved to Salt Lake City, our daughter and son handled the pressure in different ways. Our son didn't respond well to the Mormon pressure. As he and his peers approached their "young teen" years, at which time Mormon boys enter the priesthood, they'd strongly encourage Mike to join the priesthood. When Mike would say "No," their response would be something along the lines, *"What's the matter with you? Don't you want to become a god, someday?"* (The goal of all Mormon males is to become the god of their own planets, in the afterlife – the Celestial Kingdom – and with their heavenly mothers [their multiple wives] create a population of soul babies to populate that new planet.) Mike's reaction was to become more and more withdrawn from the general community. Our daughter Linda knew where she stood in her Christian faith, accepted Mormon friends and "dished it back" as quickly as they "dished it out" to her. She'd even teach her friends Christian songs like *"Jesus Loves Me,"* during lunch break in the school cafeteria. One time, she was walking into the seminary with her friend, wearing her cross necklace on a chain. A boy reached out and flipped up that cross, saying to her, *"Your faith is in that pagan symbol."* She retorted, *"Your faith is in your underwear"* (Mormon garments). She was secure in her faith and self-esteem, and handled herself well. In Pocatello, the pressure was not as intense, though one time, Linda did not make it onto an elementary school cheer leading squad because she was of the wrong faith.

It was in Pocatello, that my counseling ministry, and one-on-one ministries, began to take shape at a serious level. I became a counselor to a number of members of the L.D.S. faith because it was my experience that they have almost no one to turn to for competent and confidential help. That religious organization has no professional clergy. Their bishops come from most any career background: grocery store managers, insurance agents, auto dealers, farmers, etc., who were chosen to be the spiritual guides of the various Ward houses. They've had no systematic theological training, or advanced educational opportunities for learning how to counsel folks dealing with genuine struggles with issues of mental stress and confusion, or personal and interpersonal relationships, etc. The woman next door to us landed in a hospital mental ward every few months. She was not mentally and emotionally equipped to raise five children, without any help from her husband. The counsel she consistently got from her bishop was that if she would just be a good mother, and be a dutiful wife and obey her husband, she'd be well. To compound the problem, too often, the professional psychologists and counselors, who were Mormon, would basically tell their Mormon clients the same thing: If they'd just be good church members, their problems would go away. Compounding the dilemma, it was not unheard of for the professional counselor to tell the bishop about his client's problems; and the bishop had no qualms about sharing that confidential information with others in the Ward. The upshot of that was that I became a "go to" person who was safe, dealt confidentially with information about clients, and had knowledge and skills in counseling.

The issue of L.D.S. women considering leaving "The Church" was a big enough one in southern Idaho, that one psychology professor at Idaho State University developed a sideline counseling practice that dealt exclusively with helping Mormon women transition out of "The Church" into an open society for which they were not prepared. The constant issue that confronted me was the untenable position in which the Mormon woman found herself. On the one hand, she had, deep down inside her, this feeling that she was a real, fully complete human being in her own right. It was the undeniable sense that she had innate value and the right to make choices without dependence upon any other human. But the religious culture taught her the opposite. In that culture, her husband is literally her god in that her eternal life depends upon his willingness to give it to her. She could not get through the curtain of death into the realm of eternal life, unless, after she dies, her husband chooses to call out her temple name. A variation on that theme is that she cannot rise out of the coffin on the other side of death unless the husband chooses to take the veil off her face that was placed there as her body lies in the coffin. If she nagged him too much, or burned the biscuits one too many times, he just might conveniently forget her temple name and she would be stuck in that casket forever, or, existing in the anteroom of the kingdoms, never to be called into life eternal. That was good leverage to keep her in line during her earthly life. Further, if she doesn't have a husband, or, at least has a male relative who will vouch for her, she can never enter the Celestial Kingdom – the highest and most fulfilling of the eternal kingdoms. She would be condemned to one of the lower servant kingdoms forever. An additional pressure laid upon the woman is that if she responds to her own sense of personhood and rebels against this manipulative structure that is permanently stacked against her, she could lose her children, her friends and social standing in society, and her only chance at salvation, albeit a second class salvation.

An **important learning**, a reminder really, at this stage of my counseling, came to me from a psychology professor at Idaho State University, who had a counseling practice on the side. I forget the exact words he used, but the gist of it was that our human bodies and minds were made to be well, and are designed to keep us that way. That concept should be a given; but often times, we fall into the trap of believing that our bodies are our enemies and seem to want to be sick, to be inclined to become diseased as a natural part of their makeup, and that our minds tend to want to devolve into one mental illness or another, one depressive mode or another, becoming a negative power against me that I can never overcome. But this professor got me to considering a variety of realities from a new angle that built a case for wellness as the norm. When our bodies are invaded by a bacterial infection, our bodies "rally the troops." They raise our temperatures to give us a fever, not to make us sick, but to kill off that bacterial infection that has invaded our bodies. Those bacterial invaders don't survive elevated temperatures well. When my finger is invaded by a splinter, if it's not removed, my body rallies white cells around the foreign object with what we commonly call pus, to protect my flesh from that invader. When a bone is fractured, my body causes me such pain that I will not use that bone, which would cause further damage, until it heals, at which point the pain goes away. No medical doctor ever heals a patient. They remove the invader, the foreign object, dead tissue or disease, which causes bodily damage, so that the body can heal itself. If the body won't heal itself, there's nothing the doctor can do to make it happen.

In the area of mental health, our brains will develop neuroses, or psychoses, when reality becomes too painful an arena in which to live. (These are not the same as chemical imbalances in the brain that cause such diseases as schizophrenia and bi-polar disorder.) With a neurosis, we continue to live in the real world, but we develop inappropriate responses to real world challenges. In a psychosis, the real world is entirely too painful and threatening to confront, and our mental equilibrium won't survive. So we create an alternate reality where we can live and react to stimuli that we can control. These mental symptoms are not signs of mental deterioration, but rather, responses of the brain to protect itself until it is better equipped to handle the unmanageable challenge. One typical symptom is for us to go into denial of a reality that is too painful to address. In most cases, it's the job of the counselor to help safely move the client to a place where she/he is better equipped to acknowledge the intruder – the fearful event – to take control of it by examining it, and releasing it so that it no longer subconsciously expresses itself through our unexplained actions and responses to certain daily, fear-inducing issues, that, on the face of it, seem irrational.

Sometimes, a life or health threatening event, that is beyond our rational skills to handle at present, will bury itself in our subconscious until a later time when we are better equipped to admit the issue and resolve it. That happened to me when I was a child and my mother told me that my father was a coward. Compounding the problem, even as a child, it was evident to me that she did not like men, in general, because of her own issues. Adding to that package, she occasionally told me that she wished she had birthed girls instead of boys. So I was doubly conflicted because I was a boy and I could only grow up to be a man. Added to that, I was also con-demned to grow up to be a cowardly man like my dad, who, my mother would occasionally remind me, was *"almost a man."* All of that was too much for my young mind to sort out. My brain packed it all up, with its implications, and stored it in my subconscious.

Nearly thirty years later, it was time to unload that burden. Over a period of a couple of weeks, I felt like I was coming unglued. I couldn't focus; my agitation was distracting me from the business at hand. I tried calling a couple of confidants for help. Neither was available. What was happening to me? Finally, I got into the car and drove down to a parking spot on the edge of Lake

Washington. As I sat watching the water lapping at the shoreline I pulled out my pocket New Testament & Psalms. It opened to Psalm 32, where I read, *"Don't be such a jackass, I will instruct you and teach you the way you should go; I will counsel you with my eye upon you."* Okay, the "jackass" part is mine. The RSV had it, *"Be not like a horse or a mule, without understanding . . ."* Sitting behind the wheel of my car, I broke out in laughter. God had unlocked my poor mind. It all spilled out. I was trying so hard to succeed in a number of projects, not because I believed in the projects, but because I was trying to live with enough success as a man to justify my father's many failings – as was pointed out so generously to me, by my mother. It was not my calling to justify my father; it was not my job to prove my mother wrong. My one task was to fulfill the calling of my heavenly Father, and all else will fall into place. At that moment I was set free to learn from my past, but then get on with celebrating my present and make plans for fulfilling my future. And so, again, a **wonderful learning** comes to me from my Lord, who has a most amazing sense of timing and humor. This time it was a learning about myself.

I've presided over 438 funerals and memorial services in my career. (The most funerals I ever presided over in one day, was three.) Most services are sad. Some have some humorous moments. Some are annoying, like the time three "boyfriends" argued with each other over who was the deceased woman's favorite, as each, in turn, went up and tried to lift up her body in the casket to give her a hug – until the funeral director stood guard at the casket while I gave my shortened eulogy.

Suicides are always difficult to handle. The dynamics

differ dramatically from typical deaths. On one occasion, a Seattle funeral director called me to lead a service for a young man who had committed suicide. He was a husband and father of two young boys, ages five and three. I didn't know any of them. The wife seemed to be appropriately weepy. A couple of days after the service I decided to call upon her and see how she was doing. I knocked on the door. The older boy heard me, came from the living room into the hall and opened the door. He recognized me; I said I had come to see his Mom. He pointed to the room where she was and I followed him in. She had not heard me knock. While the boys played on the floor, she was lying on the sofa wearing only the top half of some baby doll pajamas; and a young man was sitting beside her on the couch, sexually playing with her. When they saw me, he got up and disappeared somewhere in another part of the house. She sat up, put a gown on, lit up a cigarette. We made small talk and then she said to me, as she waved her hand, *"I'm going to start coming to church, but first, I need to give up these cigarettes."*

I thought, *"Yeah, those cigarettes are certainly the most important issue here."* We exchanged a few more polite words, and I left, thinking, *"I believe I now know one of the reasons that husband committed suicide."*

Dealing with folks contemplating suicide is an issue in every community. On one occasion, a middle aged Pocatello man associated with our church called me to say that he was going to kill himself. I told him I'd come over. He had no available family, and no social life outside of his employment, which was working as a hotel bellhop. People have asked me, from time to time, what are my techniques for dealing with a suicidal individual. The answer is, I have no idea. I'll play it as it goes when I get there. In the case of this man, he was trying to decide which knife to use. So I sat down and joined him in talking about the pros and cons of which knife would be the best: which would have a long enough blade, which would hurt more. Slowly I turned the conversation to his worth as a person, who would miss him, who would take over his job at work. I wondered, with him, how God would feel about one of His children doing this, and so on. After a time, he chose to live awhile longer and allowed me to take him to the psych unit of the hospital. After he got out, he called and wanted to meet me for coffee and a sweet roll. He wanted to thank me for saving his life. I really wanted to pick up the check for that table treat. I knew he had very little money. But I also knew that his self-esteem required that he be able to thank me in the best way possible; and that included paying for the goodies. Later, I was so glad that I had the good sense to keep my mouth shut and let him express his gratitude, without my ego getting in the way and ruining it for him, by insisting on paying the bill.

In Salt Lake City, a young woman called me and said that a friend of hers was planning on taking her life. She asked if I would go to her home and talk to her. I agreed to do that. This young woman welcomed me and told me her story. She was the daughter of a Mormon bishop. As she contemplated both her earthly life and her eternal life, within the Mormon context, she felt trapped by the expectations placed upon her in this life. But then, not even death was an out for her because she couldn't stand the thought of spending eternity being a "baby factory." (I occasionally teased a Mormon woman, when I thought it'd be permissible, who was complaining about her kids, by saying, *"Just think, in the Celestial Kingdom, you can't even look forward to menopause to stop birthing kids."*) The Mormon teaching is that the purpose of the woman, in the Celestial Kingdom, is to produce soul babies. These infant souls will be placed in the physical bodies of gestating babies developing in human uteruses on earth. In the teachings of The Church, the process of baby production is the same in the Celestial Kingdom as it is on earth: the woman is impregnated by her husband through sexual intercourse, and she goes through nine months of gestation before giving birth. This process goes on forever, the purpose being to populate the new planet, over which her husband has been assigned to be a god, just as heavenly Father and his heavenly mothers (wives), produce soul babies to be embodied in human form, on this Planet Earth. Polygamy is the norm in the Celestial Kingdom because it's realized that one woman cannot bear enough soul babies by herself to get the job done. One day. The Salt Lake Tribune carried an article by a BYU professor who was reflecting upon the problem of kingdom demographics. He stated that there will be more men in the Celestial Kingdom than women because the mortality rate among males on earth is higher than female mortality. This presents a mathematical problem in the afterlife, since every man in the Celestial Kingdom needs at least three wives to help him populate his newly assigned planet. His conclusion was that, mathematically, there won't be enough women in the Celestial Kingdom to provide at least three wives for every man.

In the case of this young woman, there was no room for teasing. She would take my playful observation of no relief from pregnancy through menopause, quite seriously; and that agonizing thought was repulsive enough to cause this bishop's daughter to plan her own death. (Death by suicide would keep her out of the Celestial Kingdom.) Though her deadly plan was quite serious, acting on that intention was not imminent; so I had a few days to work with her, though one day, I did have to call the police to break in and make sure she was still alive, which she was. On one occasion, she was lying on her couch and I was sitting on a chair beside her. She shifted her leg, and I started talking about what wondrous creations our bodies are – how our brains move our body parts according to what will make us more comfortable, without us even thinking about it. Then I reflected upon the marvelous intricacies of our circulatory systems, our nervous systems, digestive systems and reproductive systems – and remarked at what a tragedy it would be to kill off such a beautiful, intricately designed creation as she was, in her body.

Then she got to thinking about the irony of her situation. Here was a Christian pastor trying to save her life, while her father, the Mormon bishop, teaches that Christian pastors are disciples of Satan and purveyors of evil. I responded that I knew that in the temple, they have dramas about the Christian pastors being the Devil's disciples. *"And yet, you're the one that is trying to keep his daughter alive,"* she observed. She wondered what he'd think about that. I couldn't imagine the conflict that might create in his mind.

She had been studying for a career in journalism, while she attended college. As she moved out of the dark shadow of her immediate crisis, she chose to accept Christ as her Savior and become a Christian. She became part of a local Christian church. I had suggested a couple of colleges that had strong graduate schools in journalism, one in Columbia, Missouri, and one in Evanston, Illinois. About six months later, she wrote to me from Evanston, and thanked me for what I had done for her. I'm so thankful for all the lives that are saved, and so saddened over those lives we couldn't save. One of the lingering tragedies of committing suicide is that if you want to punish your loved ones for life, this is the way to do it. Those loved ones will blame themselves to greater or lesser extent, for the rest of their lives, wondering what they should, or should not, have done or said, so that you wouldn't have chosen to die.

I mentioned humor in a funeral service. Sometimes the humor comes from the deceased, who left some humorous instructions in his will. One was the Seattle man who left it in his will that he wanted a soloist to sing, "*I'm Glad You're Dead And Gone, You Rat, You Rascal You.*" I've had to work in "Home On The Range," a couple of times; but that song was a bit much. (Of course, I'm guessing that it expressed the sentiments of at least some of those in the audience.)

A humorous moment comes to mind concerning a service that was held in a cemetery in Seattle. I was asked to lead a graveside service for a woman I did not know. After talking with a family member I got some sense of who the deceased person had been. Since there would be no formal service, I decided to put together a meditation that would honor this wife, mother and friend, to go along with the actual committal service. This was back in the day of typewriters and black and red ink ribbons. My practice was to use the red ribbon to type all of the key words, thoughts and phrases, so that I could look up and down from my notes, with my eyes catching the important stuff that was in red type.

Because of the possibility of rain showers in Seattle, it was typical to have a canvass shelter cover over the gravesite. This cemetery used red canvass coverings rather than green. My routine is to stand at the back of the hearse and precede the casket as the pall bearers carry the casket, in this case, about 100 feet from the hearse to the grave. It turned out to be a gorgeous day with the sun shining brightly in the sky. The gravesite was prepared with the casket frame positioned over the hole, with planking around the sides, and fake grass over the planks. After the casket was positioned on the frame, I started to walk around the casket to stand at the head. Problem was, one plank wasn't in place under that grass carpet. When I stepped there, I started down into the grave. I grabbed onto the side of the casket, pulled myself up, and continued to the head of the casket. But what popped into my mind was a picture of me standing down in the bottom of that grave, trying to look dignified, while trying to work out how I was going to get out of there. It was a hilarious image to me and cracked me up. <u>However</u>, it is absolutely <u>not</u> acceptable for the pastor to break out in laughter at such a solemn and grieving moment as that. My belly was bouncing up & down as I worked at keeping the giggles contained. Next, the bright sunshine was streaming down through the red canvass cover, so that when I opened my small notebook, the red rays on the white pages, turned everything red, fading out all of my key words, thoughts, and phrases, which were typed in red. That pretty much left me with a bunch of ands, the's, and buts typed in visible black ink. Also, seeing the humor in that, I dissolved into a quivering mass of jello, out of which I had to find a way to salvage some kind of solace for that grieving family. I'm truly thankful there were no cell phone videos in that day to record those special moments.

13

Living Christianly in the Mormon Culture

SO WHAT SHOULD THE ATTITUDE and plan of ministry be for the Christian pastor and his family, when living in a community dominated by the Church of Jesus Christ of Latter Day Saints? Some Protestant clergy and Bible preachers move in with the express purpose of doing battle with the dominant church culture and all of the "evil" it represents. More often than not, they do little to convert the Mormons, and they often do harm to their own psyches. Just as our daughter did, Sandy and I chose not to fight the major culture, but to live in it, recognize it's dynamics, and rather than saying bad things about Mormonism, spend the time talking about the love of God through Christ Jesus His Son, our Savior. I never spent any time in the pulpit preaching against the L.D.S. Church, and its beliefs; I focused solely on the love of Christ, the will of God, and the challenges and means of living out the Christian Faith, wherever we found ourselves. The curiosity to me was that perhaps up to a third of our congregation was comprised of people who were ex Latter Day Saints and/or non-practicing Mormons. They participated in all ways possible in church life, supporting the ministry with money and their participation in our ministries. What many of them could not do is join the church, without seriously damaging their business and social connections, which they felt were vital for their success in those communities. The Dean of the School of Pharmacology was a participant in our congregation. He was a totally dedicated Protestant Christian; but he dare not join the church because he had to raise money in the Valley to build a new School on the university campus. He was quite sure that being a member of First Baptist Church would be detrimental to that task (which he ultimately succeeded in accomplishing).

Though I believe that my personal understanding of the theology and practice of the Christian Faith, is as close to the teachings and practices of Jesus Christ, as any I've seen anywhere else, I try hard not to judge that I am right and others are wrong, or that somehow, God hears and responds to my prayers and not to others' prayers and beliefs. And most certainly, even within my own frame of scriptural reference, I'm intentional about not judging, in my mind, that this person is going to heaven, and that one is going to hell. That is entirely up to God, and not to me – even if I do have some private opinions on the subject, from time to time. As my literary mentor, Stanley Jones, put it, *"What unites us is 'Jesus is Lord.' All else divides us."*

On one occasion, in Pocatello, I was in my dentist's chair. He was a Mormon First Counselor, who regularly listened to me on the radio, as many Mormons did, and then gave me his beliefs while he had his fingers in my mouth and I couldn't talk back. We liked each other, apart from our dentist/patient relationship. One day he asked me what I thought of the porno shop opening downtown. The store had occupied a little shop in an out-of-the-way place until recently, when the owners leased a building on Main Street, a half block from the Baptist Church to the north, and a half block from the Episcopal church to the south, and straight through the block from one of the high schools. The people setting it up decorated the front with garish yellow and purple lights and paint. They brought in strippers from Las Vegas to complement their sex products for sale. Even more concerning, they started advertising for Idaho State students to come and try out their products. I felt the owners had crossed a line.

My dentist proposed that the Protestants and the Mormons work together to get rid of that enterprise. I thought that was a good idea. I attended the next Ministerial Assn. lunch and asked everyone what they thought about taking on this project. Most agreed that I should organize something. They assured me that they were all behind me. Thing is, they forgot to say just how far behind me they were. Turns out that only the Baptists joined the Mormons, in taking on the porn parlor. We wanted to keep our demonstrations non-confronting, but effective. The Mormon leaders suggested that they gather at our First Baptist Church to make some plans and pray for God's blessing and guidance in this project. When we finished our planning, one of them suggested that we gather down front in the sanctuary where we could kneel down to pray. Thus came **another learning** my way. It crossed my mind that I certainly could not entertain the thought that God would hear and answer my prayer in that sanctuary, but would not respond to the Mormon prayers. Though I disagreed with almost everything the L.D.S. Church did and stood for, theologically and socially, I could not say that God did not hear them and respond to them in their needs. If that is indeed the case, then my business is to present the Gospel in the best way that I understand it, and let the Lord take care of the rest of it – including the Latter Day Saints. On that day in Pocatello, all of us were down on our knees praying to the heavenly Father. And ultimately, our prayers were answered in the affirmative.

We called ourselves the "Pocatello Sweepers," since every movement needs a gimmick by which to be remembered. (We euphemistically hoped to sweep the city clean.) So we each carried a broom. There's lots to be said about our experiences as The Pocatello Sweepers; I'll mention only three. First, some nearby business owners told me quietly that they were supporting us. They didn't want that kind of trash in their midst; but they would not come out publicly to support us; and, if we got into trouble, we could not depend upon their support, because it would be bad for business. This included a couple of business owners who were members of my church. So we were on our own. A second thing was that it was fortuitous that we began in the late fall of the year. We found that the worst thing we could say to those potential customers and patrons was to wish them *"Merry Christmas,"* and offer them a friendly smile, as they headed toward the back door off the alley—which was the main entrance. They were braced for harsh words, but they didn't know how to handle kindness. (They didn't want to wish us *"Merry Christmas,"* back. (Somehow, that didn't feel right, in that circumstance.) Over time, that tactic cut the customer count significantly. Finally, it turns out that this store was part of a chain of stores owned by organized crime. The woman who ran them for the mob from down in

Phoenix was not pleased when we made the national news media. She sent a couple of mobster toughs up to Pocatello, to spread the news around the streets that if I didn't back off from leading this protest, my wife and kids would be kidnapped and sexually molested. The long and the short of it was that that operation was shut down within three months and did not reopen anywhere else in the area.

It was a typical practice in Idaho and Utah for the person running the high school L.D.S. seminaries to invite Protestant clergy to come and speak to the class about their beliefs. Those clergy members, initially, including me, would go and speak to those high school youth, presenting our best arguments for why our beliefs in God through Jesus Christ were correct. We represented a variety of denominations that presented a variety of worship styles and belief systems. Most of us, in our own way, felt good about our presentations. Each of us felt that our statements were surely logical, airtight, and persuasive. We'd leave, believing that we did well to convince those students of the truth. What I soon learned was that the instructors were well versed in what we'd be saying about our various theological stances. After we each left, they'd point out that we could not all be correct, since we differed on so many points, and then, they'd reinforce their belief that they had the one true religious faith. So I worked at getting ahead of the game by picking just one or two topics. Maybe it would be the term "heavenly Father." I'd explain how they believe that heavenly Father is their biological father, since their souls were conceived by him, and gestated in the heavenly mother's uterus, before being birthed here on earth. Then, without any criticism of their position, I'd contrast that position with the Christian's understanding of ours being a spiritual relationship, in which we are created in the spiritual image of our heavenly Father rather than the physical image. I'd talk about our spiritual relationship to God, the heavenly Father, and through His Son, Jesus. Then, without judgment statements regarding which position was closest to the truth, I'd leave the subject for them to sort out in their minds for themselves.

I became a "trusted Gentile" – one who would respect them and care about them as persons, while disagreeing with their religious positions. On one occasion, I was invited to speak at the L.D.S. Institute at Idaho State University. On another occasion, after we moved south, they invited me to speak to the L.D.S. Institute at the University of Utah, both college versions of the high school seminary. At the U of U, I chose to speak on the "priesthood of all believers," which is a theological issue dear to the hearts of all Baptists. I began by reviewing the Mormon teachings on the priesthood; then I described the Baptist position on the priesthood. From there I moved to the Latin derivation of the word, in which the word *"priest"* means *"bridge"* – the priest is a bridge that provides a way across a gulf of righteousness to God. Then I continued by talking about our responsibilities as "priests" to be humble servants who invite others into the presence of the heavenly Father, rather than living with pride over holding the title of some "office" in the Church. It turned out to be a rather well-received message, with a lot of genuinely sincere compliments offered, afterwards, which is a bit unusual, since there is no room in the Mormon belief system for grace.

One of the great debates between Christian theology and

Mormonism is the confrontation over whether or not salvation comes through "faith" or "works." The *"proof text"* for the Christian's "salvation through faith," is Ephesians 2:8-9: *"For by grace you have been saved through faith; and this is not your own doing, it is the gift of God—not because of works, lest any man should boast."* (RSV) In contrast, the "proof text" for the Mormon's position favoring "works" is James 2:14-17: *"What does it profit, my brethren, if a man says he has faith but has not works? Can his faith save him? If a brother or sister is ill-clad and in lack of daily food, and one of you says to them, 'Go in peace, be warmed and filled,' without giving them the things needed for the body, what does it profit? So faith by itself, if it has no works, is dead."* (RSV)

The theological arguments can go back and forth endlessly, with no satisfactory outcome. Then it hit me one day: We Christians are arguing theology when the real argument centers on psychology. The Mormon cannot depend upon grace. In fact, it's quite the opposite: He must spend his life proving his adequacy and lack of dependence upon others, including Heavenly Father. Why? Because his goal in life is to prove that he is worthy of godhood. His great goal is to go before the council of gods in the Celestial Kingdom and prove that he is, through his works, worthy of being assigned a planet somewhere in the universe, where he will be named its god. If he depends upon Heavenly Father's grace for his salvation, he's demonstrating that he's not strong enough and resourceful enough to be worthy of godhood. Regarding Heavenly Father, reigning over the planet Earth comes the well-known L.D.S. saying: *"What man is, god once was. What god is, man may become."* Heavenly Father was once a male human, as some of us are, on another planet, and was a good enough human being that he was awarded godhood over planet Earth long ago. In the meantime, the Mormon woman has to work hard enough in the Relief Society, teach enough classes, bake enough casseroles for the sick and bereaved, that she'll be worthy of being a Heavenly Mother in the Celestial Kingdom. When I would ask a Mormon if he/she was "saved," or would make it into the Celestial Kingdom, the common answer would be, "*I hope so.*" It's a mindset. Each hopes that he/she has accomplished enough good works to qualify. But in all of that, there is no room for salvation by God's grace, through the sacrificial love of Christ upon the cross. (You never see a cross on, or in, a Ward House or Stake House, or as jewelry around a person's neck.) The ultimate question for the member of the Church of Jesus Christ of Latter Day Saints is not, "*What has God done for me through Grace,*" but "*Have I done enough to prove myself worthy?*"

On the occasion of "the Prophet's" 80th birthday, Sandy and I were officially invited to the banquet honoring President Spencer Kimball. We received some very nice china and mementos of that occasion. On another occasion, I was invited to the Tabernacle on Temple Square when President Jimmy Carter was stopping for an official visit. I had a good seat, close to the front. Apparently, I was the "token Gentile."

One rule that must be observed by every visiting dignitary from around the world who comes to Utah, is that you may visit the Governor to pay your respects, if you choose, but you <u>must</u> visit the "the Prophet" and the Church dignitaries. So while we honored guests in that jam-packed Tabernacle waited as the Church leaders and the Governor went out to the airport to escort the

American President into Salt Lake City, we were entertained by Marie Osmond and The Osmond Brothers, who were very popular performers, nationally, in that day. Then, what caught my attention was that when the Presidential party arrived, with all of the religious dignitaries, President Jimmy Carter was ushered up to the front of the Tabernacle, where there was a seat for every important dignitary – everyone, that is, except Governor Scott Matheson, who had to go, by himself, up to the balcony and ask a couple of folks to scoot over a bit, so that he could sit down on the end of a bench. Ah, only in Utah . . . you've got to love it: This Baptist minister was given a better seat than the Governor of the state.

The most surprising moment of ministry came to me when a representative of a group of Mormons, who regularly come together at the time of the annual Conference, came to me and asked me to speak to their group. My topic was to be one of my choosing, in which I was to criticize the Mormon Faith. I was speechless. I tried to think of any way that we Baptists would invite an outsider, who is basically antagonistic to our Faith, to come to speak to us at our Annual Gathering about what's wrong with us. But the premise of the committee was that they live isolated lives – geographically, if they live in Utah, and in any case, spiritually, as they live out their lives in their closed society. They trusted me, believing that I would not just attack them out of my prejudices. They wanted to see themselves through my eyes, so that they could be better people through constructive criticism; and they knew that whatever I said, I would say in love. I finally agreed to take on the project after being assured that the audience would be well informed that this was not my idea; I was following the wishes of the program committee.

So we gathered at the Hotel Utah, where I chose to speak on *"Why Joseph Smith Fails The Test"* (of being a prophet, based upon the teachings of the Mormon Church, itself). I was amazed that I received a standing ovation at the end of my presentation. A second shocker for me came when I was invited back to the banquet the following year, just to have fellowship with them. Everyone at the table said, *"Oh, you're George Nye. You spoke to us last year on 'Why Joseph Smith Fails The Test,'" and you said . . ."* this, and this, and this. I was flabbergasted. They were right on. I laughed and told them how amazed I was. I said that my own Baptists can't remember my Sunday sermon beyond Sunday afternoon dinner.

14

Struggles with Ministry in the Heart of Zion

OUT-OF-STATE FOLKS would often ask me, *"How do you get along with all of those Mormons?"* My response would invariably be, *"It's not the Mormons that are the problem; it's the Baptists that give me fits."* I offer that response with only a smidgeon of humor and a large dose of reality.

The dynamics that rule in a Christian church in the Salt Lake Valley are different than the dynamics that define life and ministry in other Christian churches across the country. I got to the point that I would tell people who wanted to understand ministry in Zion, that people suppose that moving to Utah is like moving to any other state in the Union, with its own set of peculiarities that could be said of any state. Then I'd say that they'll better understand what it's like if they think of the experience as moving to another nation – like moving to Japan or Ecuador, or Singapore. One lives in the foreign culture that dictates a whole variety of human interactions; but one doesn't expect to convert that whole culture. One accepts that he/she will live a minority lifestyle in the midst of the rules, attitudes and values that will be in contrast to one's own priorities and guides for living.

The Christian church becomes a refuge in an alien land. That feature of life in Utah brings in a number of folks who would otherwise not attend church; but that's a mixed blessing. For example, a young family moved up to Salt Lake City, from the Los Angeles basin. The husband's company transferred his job to Utah. The family consisted of a wife and husband and three kids. They had been very involved in church and Youth For Christ in southern California; and they had agreed that they would take a hiatus from church, when they moved to Utah. They had decided that they were "burned out" on church life and youth ministries. However, within two weeks of their move to the Beehive State, they showed up at First Baptist Church, Salt Lake City. The Mormon pressure on their kids was too great to ignore. They, of course, were welcome; but they were not happy about being there. They were not a positive influence on church life; and they were not prepared to get involved in the ministries of the church, other than to attend programs that ministered to their children.

This unusual connection to the church in Salt Lake showed up in a variety of ways. For example, at one point, early in my ministry there, we needed to replace some of the bar tiles on the church roof. It was going to cost enough money that we needed to hold a congregational business meeting to vote in favor of the financial expenditure. It was going to be even more expensive because I could not find a Utah roofer to do the job; so we would have to bring a roofer I knew in Pocatello, down to Salt Lake City, to do the job. I scheduled the business meeting to follow the Wednesday evening gathering and Bible study. When we were called together for our evening program, I said to the moderator, *"Why don't you just call the business meeting first. It won't take more than five minutes; and we'll get the business out of the way so we can get on with the Bible study?"*

The moderator thought that was a good idea; so he got the church clerk to take notes and the people were called to order. We all agreed that the work seriously needed to be done. The money was authorized; the meeting was closed. And we got on with the Bible study. Toward the end of the study and discussion time, church members started arriving and gathering in the back of the Social Hall. As I closed the meeting, there were about forty or more people standing in the back. When I dismissed everyone, someone called out, *"When does the business meeting begin?"*

When I explained that we held it at the beginning of the gathering, rather than at the end, I was suddenly confronted with a lot of anger and frustration. *"What was going on? Why would so many people come out at 9 p.m. in the evening for a brief business meeting? Why would these folks not come out to participate in the church being the church, but would come out in the late evening to vote on a roof repair for the building?"*

Here was congregational anger that was now to be bundled with the cool resistance to ministry by people who were forced to attend church to escape the pressure of the dominant culture. When Sandy and I drove through Salt Lake City, for the first time, years earlier, as we were on our way from our wedding in Robinson, Illinois, to our first church in Hay, it was like there was something in the air. We both said, *"We're never coming here to minister."*

About this same time as I had called that "untimely" business meeting, a late 40s-aged single woman came to worship, joined our church; and looked for a place to serve. She was an Air Traffic Controller. She took the job of treasurer and did a good job. She also helped out with the youth program from time to time. Soon someone decided she didn't like her and created the rumor that she was a lesbian. As the rumor spread, members started saying that she is a danger to our youth, particularly to our girls. For the first time in my life, I strongly urged a church member to leave our congregation for her own safety. I did not want to lose her, but she did not deserve the vicious attacks that were coming down on her in our congregation. I suggested to her that she try our Baptist church over on the west side; she'd be warmly welcomed there, and they could use her talents. She did and she was warmly accepted. These were the days when I'd tell Sandy at breakfast, *"I'm going to work. If I make it to lunch, I'll give it a try in the afternoon. Otherwise, I'm going back to selling shoes."*

I reached out to my denominational leaders for guidance and support – three of them, as I recall. I got nothing, zip, not so much as a *"by your leave!"* Then, one day, Russell and Elsie Orr made the long, arduous climb up our front steps to our porch from the street below, and unannounced, rang our doorbell. Russell was now retired, and they were on their way home from Arizona, back to Seattle. On the spur of the moment, they decided to stop in and see how we were doing. Why he would decide to do that when he was suffering gout, and had to wear a soft bedroom slipper on that horribly swollen, painful foot, is beyond me, unless the Lord had a hand in it. To me, he was, indeed, a gift from God.

Dr. Russell Orr was the Executive Minister of Washington State, when I met him. He had come to the school in Berkeley, to look over the latest crop of graduating students to decide who of us might be promising candidates for his churches in the Northwest. He and I spent a long time talking, and we seemed to hit it off. I was a tarnished candidate, with that divorce in my background; but somehow, he liked what he saw and decided to take a chance on me. He set me up with the church pulpit committee in Hay. He mentored me there, from time to time, then followed me with interest in Seattle, at about which time, he retired. But, he never lost interest in how I was doing in ministry – hence, this surprise call at our home in Salt Lake City . . . even when it meant a painful climb up those 30-40 steps on that gout-stricken foot.

After they got settled in the living room, we exchanged some pleasantries and heard about their trip home from Arizona. Then, Russell asked me, *"How is it going?"* That's all it took. I started telling him. Before long, Elsie decided that it was time to retire to the kitchen to have a more pleasant conversation with Sandy. I spoke of the bewildering anger and coldness in the congregation, the struggles with issues that made no sense, the peculiar attachment the people had to the cathedral, which indeed was huge and beautiful, but offered no investment in ministry. I spoke of my own lack of ideas and insights for ministering to the people here. I must have spoken nearly non-stop for a half hour. When I finally ran out of breath and stopped talking, Russell said, "Well, all that comes to my mind to say is what the Apostle Paul said to Titus, *'That's the reason you're <u>in</u> Crete.'*"

Russell explained. The Apostle Paul had sent Titus to Crete as a young pastor, to build a Christian community there. Titus finally wrote to Paul and basically said, *"These people are impossible! Get me off of this island!"*

Paul's response was, *"Of course they're impossible. They are rebellious, empty talkers and deceivers, especially those in the church, who must be silenced because they are upsetting whole families, teaching things they should not teach. Even one of their own leaders said, 'Cretans are always liars, evil beasts, and lazy gluttons.' This testimony is true. That's the reason you are in Crete!"*

Russell's message to me was Paul's message to Titus: *"Of course these people are impossible, angry, cold people. That's why you were put here!"*

I broke out in laughter. It was a wonderful moment. I needed no further advice – no commiseration. *"That's precisely what your ministry is about. Now quit your bellyaching and get to work."* I've loved the Epistle of Paul to Titus ever since.

15

"Fort First Baptist"

MY FIRST STEP was to confront the congregation in a sermon titled, "FORT FIRST BAPTIST." What precipitated the move at this moment was a financial crisis. I went over the giving records. My tithe on my modest salary made me the third top giver in the church. Our Minister of Christian Education tithed her pitiful salary, which made her the sixth top giver in the congregation, and our daughter, Linda, tithed her babysitting money, which made her tenth top giver in the church. It was time to take a serious look at what our church is to us in the Mormon culture, and to look at changing a common image we have held of ourselves to seeing ourselves as the body of Jesus Christ in the Salt Lake Valley. The following is an infamous sermon I preached, as I joined biblical Titus and got underway with my assigned ministry.

"FORT FIRST BAPTIST"

At the height of the German attacks on England, Winston Churchill called his cabinet together in the bunker. He went to a large map on the wall to point out the enemy positions. He noted that between the German Army, Navy, and Luftwaffe, the British were pretty well surrounded, The Royal Air Force was down to 6 planes and London was nearly leveled by the nightly bombing. France was conquered, America wouldn't help; and the Germans could bomb their island at will.

Churchill was quiet for a few minutes to let the situation sink in. The Cabinet members started groaning and despairing. Some talked of giving up, surrendering their homeland. Then he quieted them and said: *"Gentlemen, I find the situation rather inspiring."* Elroy Shikles, Baptist pastor in Grand Junction, said, *"When God wants to do something, He starts with a problem. When He is going to do something great, He starts with an impossibility."*

We at First Baptist Church can identify with both of those statements. That's because we feel besieged. Some of us are hard put to find the hand of God in this crisis that has come upon us. Yet, this may be just exactly what God has been waiting for, for years to happen, so that He can act.

There's no doubt about it – we're facing the possibility of losing our church as we now know it. Some will think that's good, others, that that's bad. The goodness or badness lies not in whether or not we keep or lose our church home, but in the reason that either event occurs. Goodness and evil lie in the hearts of people, not in bricks and cinder blocks. The financial dilemma overwhelming us at the moment is not new. It's been growing for years. In fact, the crisis is not even basically monetary. It's a spiritual issue that is reflected in our physical actions. Our financial crunch is the symptom of a disease; it's not the disease itself.

To get at our problem, look at our church building: Fort First Baptist. For many it is a citadel sitting on the hilltop, a statement of resistance against the dominant culture, a fortress in a hostile land, a beachhead in an alien country. We come here to defend ourselves against the Latter Day Saints. We use the building to establish our identity. We bring our children here to keep them out of the clutches of Primary, or Mutual. We have to be assured that it's alright to be a Gentile in the land of Zion. So we duck in here to avoid the arrows of those who constantly woo us from Temple Square. We seek to reinforce our desire to be independent of the majority. We need to shout out to the community, "*I am a Baptist. I am not L.D.S!*" Other pastors have told me, after hearing of our financial problems, that we must not lose this building; for this "Baptist Cathedral" on the hill is a source of encouragement for their congregations, as well.

So everything we do is measured against what the Mormons do. We can't just build a new church home; we must build a cathedral to stand up against the temple. We can't just purchase a serviceable organ; we must buy an instrument that, if not larger in quantity of ranks, then better in quality of sound, in our need to declare it superior to the tabernacle organ. Our parlor was featured in "Sunset" magazine. We can't do Christian Education for its own sake; we must measure our teaching techniques against what they do in an L.D.S. Sunday school. As one member put it, *"We want to mimic – but not be – a Mormon in every way except in evangelism and stewardship."*

Nobody wants to live in a fortress. Our pioneer forebears wanted to live on their farms and ranches. When they came under attack by the local natives, they were thankful for the Army fort, to which they could flee for safety. They were glad to be there for their safety; but they resented <u>having</u> to be there. They wanted to be at home. In a similar way, if we <u>have</u> to be here, we resent it. We come because we feel pressured out in the community. So we accept the tradeoffs grudgingly. It makes us feel good and proud to drive up 13th East and say, *"There's my church!"* We can even see the blue light in our tower all the way downtown. So for those feelings and the safety and identity we receive, we grudgingly pay our dues. In fact, I've never before been in a church where women literally must pay their dues to belong to a circle. But it fits our pattern: Women don't give out of a loving response to the Lord's work; they give because that's what they must pay to belong.

Because of what this building represents, people will respond generously for its upkeep. How often trustees will point out that we've never had trouble raising money for building maintenance. But we will not pay to maintain the ministries of the church. Why? Because a number of us aren't here primarily for ministry. We're here to maintain the fort. In this case then, our pledges are dues. They are not loving responses to a God who calls us to be his children. They're tax deductions, not offerings of compassion to the lost sheep of Jesus' flock.

This building should be a tremendous witness to the Salt Lake Valley, standing for the love of Jesus Christ. To some on the outside it is a beacon of hope. Ironically, to some on the inside, it's an idol – a shrine to its own glory – and to our pride. To others, it's the citadel, a place of refuge. If we are to save our church – and save our souls – we must turn from a fortress mentality to seeing our church for what it is supposed to be: A witness to the gospel of Jesus Christ and a beacon of hope in a dark world. We are to be that light, set upon the hill that cannot be put under a bushel . . . piercing the darkness and hopelessness. We're to be a symbol of the hope in Christ that is more powerful than the aimlessness and cynicism that overwhelms much of life. It's not that we cannot meet our stewardship obligations; it's that we've seen fit not to. There are 231 giving units in this congregation. If just 130 units tithed on an average annual salary of $15,000, our total church income would be $195,000. That's $70,000 more than we've budgeted. It's not as if we're "*dreaming the impossible dream;*" it's only a question of reassessing our personal priorities.

E. Stanley Jones laid it out for us in no uncertain terms when he said, "*Get out of yourself or perish.*" We are at a crisis point, there's no denying it. We could lose it all, and that's not just scare talk. But we don't have to. We'll lose it all if we insist on being a dues-paying club, or a Mormon-resisting fortress. We will gain the glory of God, and victory through the Holy Spirit, if we are willing to become the Church of Jesus Christ.

John lines it out for us: "*See what love the Father has given us, that we should be called children of God.*" If we're here on any other basis less than an enveloping love of God, we're missing completely what Christianity is about. John goes on: "*God is greater than our hearts, and He knows everything. We receive from him whatever we ask, because we keep his commandments & do what pleases Him. And this is His commandment, that we should believe in the name of His Son Jesus Christ, and love one another.*" To be the church, and in communion with our Lord, it must be our aim to "please God" in what we do, say, think, each day . . . and to believe in His Son Jesus Christ . . . and to love one another; this is the mark of the Christian.

As Joshua approached the people who stood at the crossroads, so must we now make a decision. They had been led to the Promised Land. Now, what gods would they serve? Would it be the local gods, or the Lord God? Victory can only come through complete commitment to the Lord God. So we stand at the crossroads, and the message comes to us just as strongly: "*Choose you this day whom you shall serve . . . the gods of brick and stone and gold leaf . . . the fortress? Or shall it be the Lord God?*" May I call you today to choose life? When you do, you will celebrate with your time and your dollars and your devotion to the God who loves you.

End of sermon.

Actually we did begin to turn that huge ship around and

head in a different direction. I also changed my attitude at one crucial point. Instead of resenting folks for being in church for the "wrong reason," I developed the attitude that worked itself out along the lines of, at least in my head, "*Glad you're here. While you're with us, do you mind if I tell you about this guy named Jesus?*" I'm guessing that my attitude change helped affect the attitude changes in the congregation as well. We became more of a community of faith and less of a club.

This is *an aside*: I've found that the Lord has a wonderful sense of humor. Even in the times of great stress, He'll give us something to laugh about. Next door to the church is the Sarah Daft Home. It was an old mansion that had been converted to a senior living community for women, with several one-room apartments, each with a bathroom, plus a common dining room where the residents received their meals. In those days, there were no other services to the residents. There were no caregivers to help residents with their individual needs, for example. I decided to stop by about 1 p.m., to visit one of our elderly parishioners. When I knocked on her door, she called out for me to come in. She was in her bed, with her right foot sticking out from under the sheets. She was suffering from gout and her foot, and her big toe in particular, were swollen until they looked like they were ready to burst. The pain was so great that she couldn't stand the pressure of the sheet on that toe. I didn't have to ask how she was doing; but I did ask if there was anything I could do for her. She said that she really had to go to the bathroom, but she couldn't get there because of the excruciating pain in her foot. I asked if she'd like me to carry her to the bathroom. "*Oh, please, would you?!*"

So I gathered her up in my arms and carefully carried her into the bathroom, and got her and her nightgown, settled down on the toilet. I left so that she could take care of the matter at hand; then got her back up in my arms to carry her back to bed. Once she was settled we talked then we had prayer together, I told her I'd come back in about four hours, on my way home to dinner, to help her again, if she still needed me. I did stop back; but the manager of the home had worked out a way to take care of her problem.

The next day I dropped by to see how she was doing. Two other church members, also residents in the Home, were visiting with her. One of them was Louise, a stereotypical "little ol' lady" with lots of giggles and a sparkle in her eyes. One never knew what was going to come out of her mouth, next. When I arrived, our bed patient began telling her friends what I had done for her, the day before, saving her from a terrible predicament, by getting her out of her bed and onto to the toilet. When she finished her story and her expressions of appreciation for her pastor, Louise clapped her hands and blurted out, *"Oh! I wish I was sick in bed so he could do that for me!"*

That brought laughter to my heart and a smile to my lips for a long while after that day. *"Thank you, Lord, for the gift of laughter."* What could be a greater dream come true than to have your pastor carry you in and set you down on the toilet?!

The congregation of First Baptist Church, Salt Lake City, had some remarkable congregational members. Some of the senior citizens in the congregation included Dr. E.R. Huckleberry who was a company doctor for most of his life. Early in his career, he worked for a logging company in the forests of western Oregon. On one occasion, a logger, wearing his crampons, was up high in an old growth tree, cutting the top out of it before falling the remainder of the tree for lumber. With his safety strap around the tree, it's close quarters trying to cut through that trunk. His crosscut saw slipped, while he was sawing and he cut open his belly. He was having to try to hold his bowels in place. Doc Huckleberry was called in and apprised of the situation. He put on crampons and also climbed that tree with what supplies he thought he'd need. He decided that the man would die if he were lowered down in that condition. Without any anesthetic, he got everything back inside the logger's abdomen, pulled his outer skin together and stitched him up. Doc said he lived, but he walked stooped over for a while until he got his belly skin stretched out again.

Later, Doc became the company doctor for Kennicott Copper, in the Salt Lake Valley, which is when he joined First Baptist Church.

Then, there was Jean Thomas, who came west, as a child, in a covered wagon. Later she went on to become a speedboat driver in boat races. She also gave many volunteer hours to women's ministries in the church.

James Barlow was a third man who deserves attention. He was a British medic in World War I. When he came to the United States at the close of the war, his credentials were not accepted for him to be licensed as an M.D. So he went into medical research. In the end, he did all of the rhesus monkey studies at the University of Utah, under the direction of Jonas Salk who did his work on the east coast. James' task was to develop a serum to use in vaccinations to prevent polio. Since he could not ship those successive experimental vials of liquid by mail, he had to carry them on his lap in commercial airplanes back east for Dr. Salk to study.

As mentioned elsewhere, another participant in the life of the congregation was Dr. Hiner, the Dean of the School of Pharmacology.

Finally, one more must be mentioned, among several others who could be mentioned. At the time of his death, Bob Ottum was a Senior Writer for "Sports Illustrated." He had recently returned home from covering the Winter Olympics in Sarajevo for his magazine. He occasionally mentioned me in his newspaper articles – one time for a sermon he especially liked. On another occasion, he declared my beard the sexiest beard in the Salt Lake Valley. In 1986, it was my sad honor to return to Salt Lake City to officiate at his memorial service at First Baptist Church. Other folks were successful business people, educators, and folks who were success-ful in law enforcement, research and medicine.

16

Developing Additional Ministries in Utah

EVEN IF ADULTS CAN, at least theoretically, develop a larger world-view, our children and youth know only what is in close proximity. Therefore, our Christian kids and youth in Utah were always painfully aware of their minority status in the community and in their schools. So when several of our women began to consider some of the greater ministries of American Baptist Women, around the nation, they came across the Guild Girls. It was a women-sponsored ministry to the girls in the church. The Guild Girls was organized on the general plan of the American Baptist Women; but the organization was age appropriate. A few Salt Lake First Baptist women got excited by the program. Karen Carter, in particular, began to imagine the possibilities. This organization was in addition to the youth program of the church. One of the greatest blessings to our girls came when they attended the national Guild Girls conference at our national conference center, The American Baptist Assembly in Green Lake, Wisconsin. Besides the excellence of the program, the mere chance of our Utah girls to participate with hundreds of other Christian girls their age, from all over the country, gave them a sense of identity, belonging, and empowerment, that they carried with them back to Utah. It provided a tremendous boost to positive feelings about themselves, and the power of their faith.

Another ministry in Utah into which a few of us pastors breathed some life, was the Ecumenical Ministries of Utah. A fact of life for all of our denominations was that regardless of our religious affiliations, none of our judicatories had headquarters, or even outlying offices, in Utah. We American Baptists had our Regional office in Seattle. As I would try to get our denominational executives in our national headquarters in Pennsylvania to understand, that's as great a distance as it is from Rhode Island to Illinois. The result was that it was not uncommon to find myself in an exchange something like this: *"When I request a missionary speaker in Salt Lake City and you respond that we shouldn't need one because you just sent one to our Regional headquarters in Seattle, that's like telling folks in Chicago, you recently had a speaker. Just last week we sent a missionary presenter to Providence, Rhode Island."*

Whether we were Presbyterians or Methodists, Lutherans, Baptists, or Disciples, we all faced the same dilemma. Like I had to rely on a retired executive who happened through Utah, to give me the direction I needed; in like manner, other pastors experienced much the same in their denominations. So we upgraded the structure and purpose of the Ecumenical Ministries of Utah, contacted each of our judicatories and told them that we were willing to be their onsite representatives. They could work through us to troubleshoot, support, and give guidance, as requested, to their local congregations. They all pretty much bought into it.

It worked well. In Layton, there was an American Baptist Church that was still accepting mission aid from the American Baptist denomination to pay its bills. A Presbyterian pastor came, assessed their situation, and told them it was time for them to grow up and stop being a mission receiving church, living on welfare. They needed to stand up *"on their own two feet"* and carry their own weight. And they did it. Down in Sandy, a Methodist church was trying to get Conference to approve a building expansion project, and their DS from another state was not giving them support in this project of ministry enhancement. I went down, heard their story, studied the situation, and laid out carefully why this expansion project was necessary to allow their congregation to grow. My onsite, (but outside) voice got the project approved. Sometimes, one of us would get called to go into a congregation and work out a conflict resolution between the pastor and the people, or step in between a couple of warring groups in the congregation and get them to begin speaking to each other, and to learn the art of compromise that will come out as an advantage to both sides. What I learned in Utah, in developing the art of mediation, served me well in Oregon when I got called in to be the mediator in several difficult situations between pastor and congregation, or between present pastor and former pastor (memories of which reinforced my decision to obey my Code of Ethics, and leave the Eastwood congregation when I retired as pastor).

In other ways, the spirit of the congregation began growing. We expanded our ministerial staff; we held talent nights, and the congregation organized a Pastor's Roast, in which I was the butt of all the humor. It went over quite well. (The man who mimicked my mannerisms was getting roars of "knowing laughter" from the people, although I couldn't see what was so funny.) We began to reach out to join in downtown ecumenical ministries in an effort to meet the needs of the homeless and those who required a leg up in order to get back on their feet. Our Sunday attendance also started growing. Just before I arrived on the scene, that congregation was down to 75 on a Sunday morning for worship. When I arrived, it soon rose to about 125 people attending worship in a sanctuary that seated 800. A few years later, we were averaging about 375 people in Sunday morning worship.

17

The Pleasure and Pain of Hospital Ministries

THOUGH I WAS CERTIFIED as a chaplain at the Swedish Hospital in Seattle, my hospital ministries did not pick up until we moved to Pocatello. Though I did not serve as a chaplain in either of the Pocatello hospitals, I did spend a fair amount of time visiting patients there, and not just members of my church. Somehow, I became known to some of the doctors and/or nurses who would call me for one reason or another. One day, a man was scheduled for surgery at the Bannock Hospital; but he was so agitated and frightened over the prospect of what he faced that the surgeon decided that the man would not survive the surgery unless he was brought mentally /spiritually under control. So he asked the charge nurse to call me and ask me to come right away to deal with that patient so that the surgery could go forward. I did come, spent about twenty minutes with that patient to reassure him of God's love for him, heard his fears, dealt with his faith in God's compassionate love, with the result that he went into the surgery at peace, and came through the procedure just fine.

On another occasion, at the same hospital, a young woman was brought in who had overdosed on drugs.

Her body was shutting down. She already had a gastrostomy tube inserted into her stomach to feed her. That Doc had a nurse call me and ask me if I'd organize a prayer group to lift this woman up in prayer, because there was nothing more, medically, that could be done to keep that young woman alive. I had a wonderful group of women who were devoted to prayer ministry, and got them quickly on board. Then I headed for the hospital to meet with this young Mom of a six-year-old boy. The current medical opinion was that she would be dead within twenty-four hours. This woman was aware of my presence, at her bedside, but there was little verbal communication between us. I talked to her and prayed over her. About eighteen hours later, the crisis passed. She was going to live. While I was standing there, the Doc came in and told the woman that she was alive, and going to return home to her son, for one reason only: prayer, and God's response to that prayer. Medical science had not saved her. She must understand that she was beyond what medical practice could do to bring her back to life. He continued by saying that she would do well to be grateful to those who prayed for her, and to God, who kept her alive, and to this pastor who had been by her side. She showed no inclination to express gratitude to any of us. About six months later, a church member was traveling about fifty miles north of town, where she lived. He decided to stop by and see how she was doing. When he introduced himself, she closed the door in his face. It was terribly sad to me that she had experienced a physical healing from the Lord, but she totally rejected the spiritual healing that was offered, that was infinitely more important.

Occasionally, it would be the patient ministering to me. I absolutely loved the folk music of "Whitewater." They were an Idaho family who had formed a band playing mountain music, and who recorded a couple of albums. The Dad played the lead and his three sons filled out the group. No group could get me more cranked up over my all time favorite, *"Orange Blossom Special,"* than they could. They'd lift me right up off the floor. Again at Bannock Hospital in Pocatello, I was called at home about 9:30 p.m. to see a patient that was in distress. When I stepped off of the elevator on the 3rd floor, there were the family members of Whitewater, in a small sitting area. The dad was quite ill and the boys had come to visit him. They had their guitars and banjo, and were sitting and talking. I greeted them and went down the hall to see the patient. After I spent time and prayed with her, I returned to the elevators. By now it was getting close to 10 p.m. It was the typical time for darkened halls, dozing off and quiet talking. The Dad said, *"There's the preacher, we'd better play something for him."* So they decided to play *"The Old Rugged Cross."* It was good, but then I said, *"That was wonderful. But, if you really want to play something for me, I'd love to hear 'Orange Blossom Special.'"* Well, that lit up their faces, and their feet started stomping, and off they went. People must have been able to hear that music in that hushed hospital, all the way to the lobby, three stories below. And before long, the night nurses were there clapping and stomping right along with them. It was one of the great gifts of my life – and especially so, since that turned out to be the last song they ever played because, next morning, the Dad died.

In contrast to the exuberance and celebration of that hospital moment, there also is a time when just the opposite, silence, is the most holy and healing time. In Seattle, one of my African American families consisted of a husband, wife, and two absolutely delightful, filled-with-personality, little girls, ages six and four. The husband/dad developed some mental health issues and became so unpredictable that he had to be barred from the home with a restraining order. One day, the mom and her girls were leaving a supermarket and walking across the parking lot when the husband approached. He pulled out a gun and shot his wife in the face, twice. The Lord must have been involved in saving that mom's life because both bullets edged around her skull without penetrating her brain. The only long-term damage done was to her hearing in her right ear. The mental damage done to those children who saw their dad shoot their mom would be profound and long term. The dad was arrested and sentenced to a residential stay in a psychiatric hospital.

Later I visited the mom in the hospital. She had to lie on her stomach because the wounds to her face were minimal; but the exit wounds were extensive and messy at the back of her skull. However bad the physical wounds were, they couldn't compare to the mental pain she was feeling – the heartbreak, the bewilderment of how her husband could do that to her, her fear for her little girls, the future . . . I uttered a few words; but they seemed inane. Words could only get in the way. I pulled up a chair beside the bed and laid my hand on her forearm, and sat quietly with her, hoping I could at least provide a physical sense of the presence of our loving heavenly Father. That turned out to be one of the most beautifully spiritual moments in my ministry. It brought peace to her soul, and a quieting to her mental agitation. After an unmeasured time, I had a short prayer for her and she fell asleep.

I remember a Bannock Memorial Hospital story that brought me some smiles. We had a member of First Baptist Church who weighed well in excess of 400 lbs. No one could be certain of her exact weight. I called on her in her home, from time to time, where she was bedridden. She looked forward to my visits. But the time came when her heart started giving out. It took two ambulance crews and two gurneys, strapped together, to get her out of bed and into the ambulance. Later, that night, I was visiting her. She seemed comatose. She needed to be propped up on one side, with pillows stuffed under her to keep her from getting bedsores. There were three nurses available, but that was not enough to role her up on her side. So I got in the middle, at her hips, and we began pushing and lifting up, which took all that the four of us had to get her up, and hold her, while one nurse positioned the pillows. All went well, and she never woke up. When I visited, the next day, she was awake. *"Pastor,"* she said, *"I had the most wonderful dream, last night. I dreamt that I had four angels lifting me up to heaven!"* I never told her who those four angels were. But I used that story in my funeral service for her, a couple of weeks later – She was lifted up to heaven in the arms of angels.

On another evening, I got a call at about 10 p.m., from a nurses' station at St. Anthony Hospital in Pocatello. One of my parishioners was having a bad time, she was frightened, and she couldn't get to sleep. Would I come? Of course I would. When I entered the room, I noticed that her roommate was softly weeping in her bed. So I spent time with my person. After awhile I prayed with her, and then, before I left the room, I stopped to see the other elderly woman who was weeping in her bed. She was quick to tell me that she was going to die soon.

That's not what bothered her. What was upsetting her was that she wanted a temple divorce before she died, because she could not stand the thought of being stuck with that reprobate, no-good husband of hers, for all of eternity. She'd much rather miss out on the Celestial Kingdom and go to the less pleasant Terrestrial Kingdom where single women and others land, than to be stuck with that husband forever, whom she so totally despised. I told her that I was friends with a First Counselor (my dentist friend), and I would ask him to get on it right away. She was grateful; and she began to relax. I did tell him; and he did get the temple divorce for the woman before she died. It's a quandary for me. I'd like to tell her that that eternal Mormon marriage business is a bunch of hooey. But I don't believe that it's wise to try to dismantle a person's lifetime faith just before she is going to die. What I did do was talk to her about how much her heavenly Father cares for her and how he will give her safety and comfort, as I reassured her of his love. And that's how I prayed for her. That was a releasing moment for her. She settled into her pillow in a resigned peace. But what made me sad was that her faith required her to choose to settle for less than the best, rather than to claim the high prize of eternal life in God's heavenly home, because of the miserable life that she imagined she would have to endure, birthing soul babies for a despised man, for eternity. I thought of that in contrast to the celebrations we anticipate through our Savior, Christ Jesus, when we enter into the glorious, loving presence of our heavenly Father, the Lord God Almighty.

I have no illusions of my own powers or importance. I do give thanks that my countenance is enough, on some occasions, to represent the presence of our loving Lord.

One evening, in Medford, I was called to the hospital ER, to see a woman who was so agitated that she would not let any healthcare professional touch/examine her until I came to see her. I didn't know her. Her husband attended the church of which I was the pastor, though she had never attended. But the moment I walked through the curtains and she saw me, she began to settle down. I took her hand and prayed for her, and that was all she needed. The hospital folks could have their way with her body from that point on. I marvel at what the presence of the Lord, working through a human, will do for people in their extremities. I visited her a few more times, in the next couple of weeks. Not long after that she died . . . at peace.

It's been my task, or privilege, to be with many folks while they died. Early on, I thought of death as a momentous moment; but it's not. It's the emotion that leads up to the death that is the big issue. Death, itself, is almost inconsequential: His heart beats, it doesn't beat. She takes a breath, she doesn't take a breath. That's about it. It's the feelings and emotions that precede that death moment that can dramatically affect the patient and/or the loved ones. Those emotions can include fear of the unknown, guilt, despair, abandonment, broken love that has spanned decades, which can fuel the anxiety. On the other side, which is best of all, there can be love's sweet and gentle grief at the impending separation, or maybe it's a sense of peace and closure, surrounding a life well lived and is now concluding, that reigns over all present, with a confidence in the life eternal that is soon to come.

My roles differed between being a pastor in one setting, and a chaplain in another. As a chaplain, I provided a short-term spiritual presence. I typically did not know the patient and family before the hospitalization, and seldom had a connection with them after they left the hospital. As a pastor, I had a long-term relationship that was multi-faceted. Each role had its own set of interpersonal dynamics. Another issue that was brought into play was whether the patient had a religious faith, or not. Occasionally, as death neared, if I broached the subject of their belief in God and their faith in Christ as their Savior, one patient might have a blank look on his/her face; another would have a flash of anger and dismiss me with suddenly closed eyes. Yet another person would want me to help them make sure that they were secure with the Lord in their faith. On one occasion a person at the nurses' station called me at home, asking me to come and baptize a man who was near death in the ICU. I grabbed my wife's candy dish (my traveling baptismal font), and headed for the hospital. I asked the nurse for directions to the patient. There was no family present, so I asked the nurse to be present as a witness. I was able to arouse the patient and told him I was a chaplain and I understood that he had requested to be baptized. *"Do you want to be baptized?" "No!!"* he said, in anger. *"You don't want to be baptized?" "No!!"*

With that, he closed his eyes and turned away his head. I questioned the nurse. *"I thought he had asked to be baptized."* She said that it wasn't him who wanted it; it was his family that had called and asked for it. Okay, so that was it. And they hadn't bothered to show up for the event. What a sad family situation that was.

On the other hand, I have marveled at the strength of the human spirit when a dying person will hang on for hours, staying alive until a loved one can get there to say goodbye. And, within a few minutes after that special person arrives, the patient can let go and slip away. On another occasion, particularly if I am a chaplain, I would hear last confessions. In some cases, the confessions had to do with some serious issues. On other occasions, I couldn't imagine such a small issue having such a profound impact upon that person's life; but it was significant to that person, and must be resolved with God before she/he dies. So again, it was my privilege to help facilitate that spiritual moment for a person at the end of her/his life.

One of the saddest experiences I had was when I was a chaplain at the regional Primary Children's Hospital in Salt Lake City. A baby was born to a new mother at a hospital in Idaho Falls, and was very sick. The decision was made to fly mother and newborn to Primary, in Salt Lake City. When the mother was told that her baby was going to die soon, she wanted the baby baptized. I headed to the hospital with my candy bowl. Though my personal beliefs told me that baptism was not necessary for this newborn to end up in the arms of Jesus, it was important to this grieving, frantic mother that her baby be spiritually covered. My job was to comfort and minister to that heart-broken Mom in the best way that I could, and that included reassuring Mom that her baby was spiritually safe. After the baptism, the nurse asked the Mom if she would like to hold her baby while he died. It might take ten minutes, maybe a half hour. Yes, she absolutely wanted to do that. We retired to a sitting area. In a little bit, the nurse came in with her stethoscope. Yes, the heart was still beating. About ten minutes later, she came back. The baby had died. The nurse would take him, now. No, the Mom wanted to hold him for just a few more minutes. As we sat there, I watched the Mom's face turn harder and more obsessive. After a couple of minutes, I motioned to the nurse and went over to take the baby's body. She wouldn't give it up. Finally, I had to literally pry her arms open so that the baby could be removed. The Mom was inconsolable; and after what I had just done, I could give her no comfort. I heard later that she would go to the grave and sit for hours at a time. Even back home, she could not let go.

One of the typical problems with family visitations that is not easily solved is that visiting family members will talk over the patient and not to the patient. They will visit with each other and not pay attention to the sick or injured person. The worst offense committed by visitors is to suppose that the patient, who seems to be unresponsive, does not hear what others are saying. It was common for me to inform the visitors that the last sense of the patient to go is the hearing. That person may not be able to talk, may not be able to see, but she/he can hear. So when visitors say to each other, *"I think he's about gone." "I can't imagine that she'll last through the night. "I'm glad this will soon be over. I've got to get home and go back to work,"* they can be doing terrible damage to the mental state of the patient.

One day, a retired judge's family had gathered. They were carrying on, back and forth, and saying some inappropriate things. I warned them to cut back on their conversation. Though the judge was unresponsive, it's quite possible that he heard them. Later, I returned to the hospital to see how the patient was doing. The room was now empty of visitors, and he was still unresponsive. I greeted him, pulled up a chair and sat down by the bed, near his head. I pulled out my pocket Testament and started reading some scripture. It felt about like I was reading to the bed stand. Then I looked up. His facial expression had not changed, but there was a tear coming out of his eye and running down his cheek. He was in there, he heard me, and he understood. When you're in the hospital room, never say anything you don't want the patient to hear, even when that person is comatose.

The hospital is a world set apart from normal life. The rules by which we typically live, don't apply in the hospital setting. For one thing, the patients are mostly naked, wearing hospital gowns that are marginal, at best, in their covering of our modest parts. Strangers come into the room to probe, palpitate, stick and penetrate our bodies at will. Beyond that, our worlds suddenly shrink down to the size of the hospital campus, and then, more specifically, to the size of our room, for the remainder of our stay. So rules of living and social norms that typically govern our actions in the outside world, don't rule in the hospital. For example, where else would I celebrate with a church member, that she just passed gas. But, after she has had bowel surgery, one of the most important of all post surgical activities is to pass gas. It's the primary indication that our digestive system is back up and running. And, quite seriously, that very good news is well worth some celebration of the first gas passed . . . in the hospital, not in someone's home or the church sanctuary.

With that in mind, one of the funniest experiences in the hospital happened on the day that I took my teenage daughter, Linda, to work with me because it was "Take Your Daughter To Work" day at her high school. We did several things that I no longer remember, as I tried to explain why this task, then that one, was important.

Then we went to Holy Cross Hospital in Salt Lake City, where I needed to see a post surgical patient who had just been told that her surgery went very well. When we entered the room, she was exuberant. *"Pastor, I'm going to get well!"* And with that she threw back the sheet and pulled up her gown to show me her abdominal incision. We celebrated her good news, and we had a prayer of thanksgiving. After we got down the hallway, Linda couldn't contain herself anymore: *"Dad! She pulled up her gown and showed you everything!!"*

I explained to her, *"Sweetheart, she wasn't being sexual. Her intention was not to 'show me everything.' She had been frightened concerning her surgery and what the doctor would find. We had talked about that. She thought she was going to die. But everything went better than expected and she's going to live; and she just <u>had</u> to share that celebration with her pastor. That incision was the focus of her celebration because it represented the good news that she's going to be all right. She would never do such a thing out in the world. But in the hospital, at this moment, that incision, and what it represents, is her whole world. In this moment, I represent to her, God's healing love; and in that sense, she needed to celebrate her feelings of thanksgiving."*

From Holy Cross Hospital, we headed south to St Mark's Hospital. There, we called on a man who also had surgery. When he started to pull down his sheet and pull up his gown, Linda slammed herself against the far wall, hands and arms plastered against that barrier. Fortunately, his was a knee surgery. If a pastor can't roll with that sort of thing without inappropriate emotional responses, while honoring each person's dignity, it is my opinion that he/she doesn't belong in pastoral ministry.

The ER can also be an interesting place for a pastor to serve. One night it's being called out of bed at 1 a.m. because the young adult daughter of a church member has overdosed on some street drugs, and will I please go to the ER to be with her. In this dark part of the day, it falls to me to turn her onto her side and hold the vomit pan so she won't suffocate herself with her stomach contents, as she throws up. Another late night encounter had me meeting a wife who had been in bed at home with her husband. They both were reading when a car, traveling at a high rate of speed, hit a rain drainage ditch in the street, lost control, and crashed through the brick and cinderblock wall into the bedroom on the front of the house. Bricks and mortar went flying into the room and landed all over the bed of the young couple. Some of those bits and pieces of brick and mortar landed on the face of the young woman. At the ER, I had to tightly hang on to her on the table to hold her still. The nurse was using a scrub brush to scrub the sand, grit, and small chunks of brick and mortar out of her forehead, cheeks, chin and nose – and without any pain killer. All the while, all this young lady could think about was, *"What if my husband and I had been making love just then?!"* At that moment, all I could suggest was that *"it probably would have broken the mood."*

In another ER experience, this time in Medford, the patient was a very much older woman who fell on the uneven garden steps and went bumping all the way to the bottom of those steps. Her face was full of cuts, some of which needed stitches; and her broken arm needed to be re-set and cast. She told the Doc that she could stand it as long as her pastor held her. I watched the stitching of her face, which is a procedure I don't enjoy watching. After the portable x-ray machine did its work, I watched him massage the bone into place. Fortunately, it was a simple break. Then, a nurse came in and encased her lower arm in a cast. All the while, she was able to lie perfectly still because I was able to cradle her and calm and comfort her. Again, that was one of those moments that is a privilege beyond price for me, when the Lord God allows me to participate with Him in His ministries to one of His children.

I served as an interim chaplain at the Veterans' Administration Hospital in Salt Lake City. Besides the patient need for a second chaplain in that large hospital, I knew that I was also keeping a pay slot open for the new permanent replacement, since, in government bureaucracies, job positions tend to disappear when the pay slot is not active. I held that position for several months.

The most interesting position I held in the medical arena was to be an ethical observer in Genetics and Perinatal Medicine. "*Only in Utah,*" said the doctor who invited me to accept the position, "*would a Jewish doctor invite a Baptist minister to be an ethical observer in a Mormon hospital.*" I served in that position for a little over two years, before I accepted a position as pastor of a church in Medford, Oregon. I sat in on doctors' rounds each week. We discussed cases of current pregnancies and how they should be managed. We went to the neonatal unit to look at newborns who had some anomalies, birth defects, etc. On one occasion, we saw a newborn baby girl who was perfectly formed, with well-formed hands and fingers, feet and toes. The only problem was that the feet were on backwards. They would have to be amputated and turned around and reattached.

I added some important insights to my knowledge of

unborn babies – **another learning**, if you will. One of the genetics counselors who was, herself, about six months pregnant, commented that her baby girl jumps inside her every time she's standing, waiting for the elevator. As the car approaches, a bell rings. I commented that I'd love to be her daughter's counselor when she's about eighteen, and she says, "*I can't explain it, but I have this thing about bells.*" This goes to our growing understanding of how much learning goes on in the baby's understanding of her/his world before birth. On another occasion, we went to the morgue to watch an autopsy of a baby girl who had died in-utero, and spontaneously aborted at close to seven months. She had a well-formed little body, but what caught my attention, when they cut open her abdomen, were her two tiny ovaries. Not only had she died, but since she already had all the eggs she would ever have in her ovaries, the next generation after her, had also died. That was emotionally hard on me.

I learned that I could make unpopular contributions to some discussions when I would suggest, for example, that perhaps it was in the unborn baby's best interest to have a different doctor than the Mom had, particularly when the current doctor was making medical choices that favored the mother over the baby. Another ethical challenge arose when the head of the department suggested that we needed to encourage more moms to have C-Sections because natural births didn't make as much money for the hospital; and she was afraid that our department would face cutbacks if we didn't carry our weight in producing revenue. But for the most part, our conversations revolved around problematic pregnancies. Though we had the world's first artificial heart beating in a patient in the cardiac unit, we had not yet advanced to genetic engineering, which introduced a quantum leap in ethical and moral issues.

18

A Counseling Ministry

MY COUNSELING MINISTRY took me all over the map. One day a secretary called and asked me to come to the corporation offices, quickly. The owner of the business was in trouble. When I arrived, I was ushered into the darkened office, and over in the corner, was the executive, a major businessman in the community, curled up on the floor in a fetal position. Pressure had been building up until a hostile takeover seemed imminent. We spent about an hour backing away from the precipice. Along about that same period of time, the word went around two different police departments that I was a resource and usually available on short notice. Officers would stop in, let go of their facades for a half hour or so, talk about some personal stuff, then end the session by typically saying, *"Okay, it's time to go get the bad guys."* They'd hitch up their gun belts, put on their cop faces, and head out the door. Sometimes, it would be an individual or a couple with whom I'd been working that precipitates a 1 a.m. call, and I'd find myself in a home kitchen. The dazed wife is sitting on a chair wearing only the top half of a skimpy pajama, with blood dripping down onto her torso from a bloody nose, the cuts and bruises on her face, and a black eye that is still swelling. Then her husband begins berating her for her lack of modesty "when they have company." That's the moment I have an up close and personal conversation, nose to nose, with elevated volume in my voice, as I convey what I think of that husband's actions and his methods of communication. I know that counseling protocol does not allow for that type of confronting behavior; but sometimes, the immediate event dictates the style of counseling to be used. (In the 21st century, the intervener is required to report domestic violence to the authorities. That was not the case for most of my active ministry years. It was up to me to back the people away from the threats and acts of violence, and establish a safe zone for those involved. Confidentiality rules were in full force for clergy for nearly all my years of active ministry. Whether the victim was a child or an adult made no difference. Reporting an incident was left to the pastor's discretion; and if reported, law enforcement was not quick to respond to domestic violence.)

On another occasion, I was recommended to a young mother who came into the office and asked me to counsel her six year old who had just been sexually molested by Mom's live-in boy friend. I told her I don't do child counseling; I don't consider that I have adequate skills for that. I suggested a couple of places she might try, to get help for her daughter. The Mom said that she'd tried, all over the city, to get her daughter in elsewhere. The only two credible counseling centers were booked up for several months. So after reiterating the disclaimer that I don't count myself as an expert in this area, I said I'd meet with her daughter and do my best. I wanted her to remain in the room, but say nothing during the session. On the appointed day, I hauled out my Barbie & Ken dolls, (Doesn't every office have those?), the doll furniture, some news print with a box of crayons, and she and I set about doing some playing and talking, first, to build rapport, as she drew some figures on the news print. When she ran out of ideas there, we switched to the dolls. That's when we got to the painful part – particularly when it was time for Barbie and Ken to take off their clothes and go to bed. Fortunately, the molestation had happened so recently that she hadn't had time yet to "stuff it" down into her sub-conscious. We could deal with the pain, fear, trust, self-blame, the loss of control, the violation and loss of a sense of self and personal value, before those issues slipped away into dark corners, to emerge later with much more damaging consequences. The trick for me was to deal with huge issues in the context of a six-year-old's thought processes and vocabulary. Barbie and Ken helped us a lot, by roll-playing a variety of scenarios. I did some follow-up, and feel that we probably got her passed the immediate crisis and into a more-or-less dependable safety zone. Thankfully, the child's Mom showed her significant other the door, and told him to never come back. I'm grateful that these days, we have some very competent child counselors; and I'll not have to be called in again. For, though it brings me a sense of satisfaction, when I'm able to connect with a person in a trusting relationship; at the same time, I don't ever want to put another person in jeopardy, or deal with that person inadequately, because I don't have the appropriate tools to meet their need.

My counseling clients presented with a variety of complaints. Another essential learning came in that I had to learn to carefully read body movements and facial expressions. Eyes are a great betrayer of true feelings.

One evening, a couple came in who were struggling with marriage problems. The husband was the domineering partner who aimed to take charge of our session. He launched into a speech that he had obviously mulled over quite a bit. To begin with, it was really a waste of our collective time for them to be there; they didn't have any real problems – just a few annoyances that all married couples have. They occasionally have some disagreements, but certainly nothing of threatening proportion; they both are deeply in love with each other and are committed to a marriage that will last a lifetime. He kept going for about fifteen minutes. In the meantime, I was watching his wife, who had no chance, whatever, to get a word in to the stream of words that was washing over us.

Finally, he had to catch his breath; and I broke in. I said, *"That's not what your wife is saying. In fact, she just said that she's not at all sure that she loves you. The problems between you two, right now, seem insurmountable; and she's not even sure that she can remain married to you for the rest of your lives—or wants to. In fact, she's not sure she can remain with you for another month."* Then, I looked at her and asked, *"Did I say all of that correctly?"* She said, *"Yes."*

"When did she say that!" demanded the husband.

"She said it while you were carrying on with all of your words. Her body language is non-stop; and it has some wonderful expressions. Her eyes, her facial expressions, her arms and legs, how she sits, in one position than in another, all tell a very different story than what you've been telling. In fact," I said, *"unless you stop talking and learn to read your wife's wonderfully expressive body language, your marriage has little chance of surviving."*

That couple didn't choose to come back again. I did meet with a terrified wife, soon after that. She asked me to hide her divorce papers, which I put in our church safe. Then I got her a motel room, where she could hide out from her violent husband. The problem was, she could not keep from calling her friends to tell them what was going on. That information got back to her husband. The next day, I got a call from a fellow pastor who said that a man with a gun was looking for me; but he went to the wrong church. That pastor, wanting to be helpful, told the angry husband where he could find me. Then he decided that maybe he should call me and give me a heads up that there's a man on his way across town who was planning to kill me. I thanked the pastor for his thoughtfulness. Apparently, the Lord turned this would be killer aside, because he didn't show up, much to the relief of my secretary.

An aside: This wasn't the first time I'd lived under the threat of violence. I lived under a death threat in Salt Lake City. I received a call from a Salt Lake City police detective. He said that I needed to know that there are men in the city who have vowed to kill both me, and a local rabbi. He stated that it has to be considered a credible threat. It was a member of the Ku Klux Klan who called the police department to give them a heads up about two men who were neo-Nazis, who were too violent and out of control for the KKK; so the Klan kicked them out. This Klansman felt some duty to let the authorities know the situation. The detective gave me their names and said that these men were already notifying the television stations that such vermin as I am did not deserve to live. I asked the detective what protection the police department could offer. He said that until they shoot me, there's nothing they can do.

That was helpful information. He said to be aware of my surroundings and don't sit in front of any windows with the curtains open. I told him that I'd learned that practice back in Seattle, during the racial revolution. It affects my selection of a seat in any room to this day.

Well, what to do? First, we had to review ways for our teenage children to be as safe as possible. Then what? Should I carry my shotgun into the pulpit? A shootout in the sanctuary didn't sound like a good idea. Of course, they could be waiting for me downtown and run over me with their car. Though living with a greater awareness of my surroundings, I would not reduce my ministries; otherwise, they had already won. Then I got to thinking about the American Presidents who had been shot, in recent years, even though they were surrounded by the whole Secret Service. If they couldn't keep from getting shot, what chance did I have of adequately protecting myself? Apparently, the reason they wanted me dead, along with the rabbi, is that we had appeared together, briefly, on a television news broadcast – though I couldn't remember the occasion and what was said.

At this point, I came to **a life-changing moment**, that has served me from that day to this: It came to me that I am a child of God, and I am living, day by day, under His merciful love. If God wants me dead, no one on earth can keep me alive; and if God wants me to live, there is no one on earth that can end my life. I did, and do, believe that with my whole heart. So I spent some time working that through in my intellectual and spiritual life, until I was satisfied that I believed that to be a fact and completely embraced it. At that point, I handed my life up to God, placed my Self in His hands, prayed through my commitment to the Lord that I would live fully and completely with that covenant now defining my eternal relationship with my Lord. To the best of my ability, I will not take foolish risks, I will not be cavalier in my activities and attitudes, but I will no longer concern myself with my life and death issues. I trust God to allow me to live on this earth until my life's purpose is concluded; and then, I trust He will take me home to eternity. I no longer need to worry about living or dying.

I wrote those neo-Nazis' names on a piece of paper, put that paper in my pocket Testament, daily prayed for them, and got on with my life. (After all, Jesus was quite specific in His instructions that we are to pray for our enemies.) That same personal covenant with the Lord has held me through other types of threats, including three spinal surgeries, and a heart stent implant. It further accompanied me as I wrestled a bank robber who was trying to stab me, as well as going into compromising situations as an officer of the court, where I have to deal with drug addicts with criminal pasts, while visiting in their homes. (This included dealing with a child I represented in court, whose family members were leaders in the Mexican Mafia, dealing both drugs and guns.) The only sadness in this affair is that those neo-Nazi men left Salt Lake City, went to Denver, and were allegedly the men who shot and killed a Jewish disc jockey. I have no lightly made theological commentary to make about "the why" of that tragedy.

I received my counseling clients from a variety of places. In Utah, many of my clients were Mormon. In Oregon, I was, for a time, on the Jackson County list of mental health resources. Also, some pastors referred their congregational members to me, as well as the word-of-

mouth referrals I received. I never had a big clientele,
but it was steady. The majority of my clients were adult
victims of childhood sexual abuse. As I worked with
those folks, mostly women, I realized that I had to learn
how to think as a woman, in order to more deeply
understand the trauma she experienced. I also had to
learn that, when the occasion presented itself, I needed
to try to explain what she experienced to the significant
man in her life. This was particularly the case when
dealing with rape. In the first place the man has no
equivalent experience. If another man attacks me,
knocks me unconscious or bloodies my nose, I can do the
same to him and deliver an equivalent retaliation. If I'm
not strong enough at the moment, I can work out,
strengthen myself, then go after him and even the score.
So, many men will look at the woman's plight and feel
badly, but have the attitude, "*Well, give back as good as
you got, and even the score.*" Being forcibly sodomized by
another man, gets closer to the issue (and I've dealt with
those clients, as well), but the victim can, later, come
back at his attacker and still, even the score. However, in
vaginal rape, there is no equivalent recourse for the
woman.

But it's more than that. I scarcely know how to put this
into words without sounding maudlin. It's a bit like
barbarians crashing into a private, inner sanctuary, with
no appreciation whatever of the beautiful accouter-
ments which they are destroying. Men's attacks on men
are external. However brutal, the man's interior self
remains intact. In rape, the female child or adult is
violated internally. It's damage at the core of her being.
Her sense of safety, her respect for self, her value and
dignity as a person, are damaged in the very sanctuary
where human life begins. And the mockery of that is a

terrible burden to bear.

One of the most intriguing features of my counseling ministry goes to the privilege I had of counseling three different clients struggling with multiple personalities. It takes a bright, creative person to get her/himself to the point where they suffer from this malady. One person I was most extensively involved with had fifteen partial and complete personalities, which we resolved, and/or integrated into her core being. After she entered psychiatric care, she ultimately resolved upwards of fifty partial and complete personalities. My other clients had not developed their coping mechanisms of changed persons nearly to the degree that my first client had. Observing how emergency measures of the human mind can kick in to protect itself from utter calamity is fascinating.

But then, dealing with a person suffering from multiple personality disorder introduced me to something that I had totally rejected, in the past: demon possession. For most of my life, as I read the Biblical stories about demon possession, I dismissed the term as early day attempts to identify the unusual behaviors of people who suffer from symptoms of what we, today, call mental illness. However, I learned that that was not the case. With mental illness, the person is the same person, but suffering from a disease – pretty much like a person is the same person, whether he suffers from cancer or is cured of cancer. In the case of possession, the evil being that takes over control of the body is not the same being as the person who has inhabited, and controlled, the body up to the moment of possession. A general sense of moral grounding, love (or lost love), connectedness through relationships, anxiousness about consequences, that underlies the conversation, actions, and the thinking of the mentally ill person is suddenly gone. In its place, is a being that is evil personified that is utterly devoid of an underlying sense of goodness. Even when in rebellion, the person is rebelling against goodness. (The demonic has no sense of connectedness to other humans or good will to rebel against.) One evening, that possessed person came to our home. My wife knew the person. She knew about the multiple personalities and had even witnessed a couple of the transitions; but she didn't yet know about the demonic possessions. Sandy became very uneasy when "she" entered our living room. As we carried on our conversation with "her," Sandy experienced the living room grow cold. She felt a very definite evil presence in the room. After several unsettling minutes, I asked this person to leave. After "she" left, Sandy said something to the effect, *"That was Deni's body, but that wasn't Deni who was visiting us. What just happened?"* (I qualify gender-oriented pronouns as "he" and "she" because the demon itself is asexual, taking on whichever gendered body that is currently available to it. [The demonic being explained that to me.])

My theory is that folks who are struggling with personality disorders are more susceptible to demonic invasion during the transition from one personality to another, than people who are solidly in control of their lives with a single personality that keeps mind and body under reasonable control at all times, even when they are struggling with mental health issues.

Deni wanted to be rid of the demonic presence and reaffirmed her acceptance of Christ as her Savior. She also wanted to be baptized as part of the completion of her faith statement and to "seal off" herself from the demonic. This church's baptistery was up high in the sanctuary, accessed from the second floor of the building. I had two young (strong) deacons with me to assist in the baptism that day, as well as being there to help other candidates who were being baptized. Deni was purposely placed last to enter the baptistery pool. She was very agitated as she came down the steps. We went through the necessary words of commitment. Then, as I lowered her into the water, the demonic took over her body with an explosion. Water went everywhere, including flying out, and down onto the chancel area. I had to wrestle/restrain her, and get her up the steps to where the deacons could drag her out. I told the deacons to drag her back to the dressing room and hold her down, until I could get down to the pulpit, preach a quick sermon, finish the service, and get back up to the dressing room. A number of congregational members saw what happened, but I couldn't explain it to them. For the most part, they just assumed that she slipped and fell. Since I was quite wet, it's a good thing I had a pulpit robe to cover me. One of the congregation's long time members wrote to me, after I moved to another church, and asked me to explain what happened, on that mystifying Sunday. I wrote him a lengthy letter of explanation to share with the congregation, regarding the events of that day, if he chose to do so.

When I got back up to the changing room, I straddled "her" body on the floor and demanded to know "her" name. (I had learned that to control the demonic, I had to know its name.) "She" said it was "Crystal" – Crystal standing for glass that can be easily shattered. Then "she" screamed a blood-curdling scream as I looked down into that hate filled, terrified throat.

"Why are you here?" I asked.

"I was sent here by the Father of Lies" (Satan). *"Please don't send me back. I don't want to go back. There is no caring there, no love, everything is a lie because our father is the 'Father of Lies.'"*

I felt an amazing sorrow sweep through me for this pitiful being who has no hope, no end to its miserable existence, no possibility of death—but rather, is condemned to living with lies and hatred forever. Then with a lot of vocal force, I got into her face and said, *"Crystal, in the name of God the Father, and Jesus Christ, His Son and our Savior, I COMMAND you to leave this body, NOW!!"* (I had learned, months earlier that the weapons of warfare with Satan are words. Words are the weapons in battle, not *flaming swords* or whatever.)

Then the body went limp, and, almost immediately, a dazed Deni came back into control of her body. Earlier in this saga, Deni had come into my office with the stated intention of killing me. I had to have a couple of deacons pin her to my office floor, while I got a different personality into control of the body. But all of that was passed, now. Later, she was admitted to the psychiatric unit, which got her headed toward the remainder of her mental health healing, in relation to her multiple personality syndrome. Even there, as she was being admitted, I was called up to the hospital to resolve one of her personalities that was not willing to relinquish control. Then, one day, Deni disappeared, and a new, integrated personality took over that allowed this fractured person to live a whole life until her death, a few years later. What a remarkable journey she took, from the catastrophic event where she chose to create her first new person to escape the pain, fear, and sense of failure of the person she was, when she was not yet five years old, to the day, decades later, when she returned to being a whole person.

About a year later, I was serving as pastor of the Medford congregation. I went up to the Psych Unit of the local hospital, to call upon a church member. When I entered the room, I stopped at the door and stared at the young man sitting there. With a strange look on his face his voice said, "*You recognize us, don't you?*" Yes I did: "he" was possessed. That young man, after being released, never came back to the church. I haven't had to deal with that issue since that day, and would much prefer not to, ever again. But the experiences I had in those moments of time were priceless. I'm glad I could be a part of it.

19

There Comes a Day
When It's Time to Move On

THE SEARCH COMMITTEE of Eastwood Baptist Church, of Medford, Oregon, approached me in the early summer of 1984. I felt like my ministry in the Salt Lake Valley was not completed yet, so I turned them down. In August, we were driving our daughter, Linda, to Linfield College in McMinnville, Oregon. We passed through Medford, stopping for lunch, on our way to the college. *"Want to look up the church?"* Sandy asked.

"No, that's water under the bridge," I said.

But a year later, there came a moment when I discovered that I had lost my sense of humor; and without that, I could not effectively do ministry in Utah, any longer. I had wanted to stay in Utah for two reasons. First, as pastor there, and representing that American Baptist Region, I could enjoy doing some work at the top levels of our denomination. Secondly, I was really enjoying my work as an ethical observer at the University Medical Center. In that latter position, I became a presenter at the national conference of "Strategies In Genetic Counseling," sponsored by the

March of Dimes, which I found quite gratifying. Problem was, neither of those interests had anything to do with my primary reason for living in Salt Lake City, which was to be the Senior Pastor at First Baptist Church. So what had robbed me of my sense of humor?

Another aside: When I was involved with a lot of traveling for denominational meetings, I liked to walk the downtown areas of the cities, where I spent some time. Early one Sunday, near midtown Manhattan. I got up to walk the blocks down toward Greenwich Village, before I attended the worship service at Marble Collegiate Church. I was walking south on Broadway, and was going to cut over to 5th Avenue, somewhere around 27th Street. Very few people were up and about at that hour. I turned east on a street in that vicinity and had walked passed the first building on my right, when I hit what felt like a glass wall. It stopped me dead in my tracks. Just passed me to the right, a couple of buildings had been torn down, and the empty ground had been blacktopped over, through to the next street.

I looked down the street I was on, toward 5th Avenue, and saw no one in the street or on the sidewalk. I tried again to walk forward. Bam! That invisible glass wall was there. I could go no further. I decided that there must be some danger down that street that I could not see; and the Lord was keeping me from going any farther. So I turned around, walked back to Broadway, headed south one more block, then turned and headed east. I had no problem. Then I noticed a local man who was on my street and cut through the block on that blacktopped area. I stopped to see what would happen. He stepped onto the sidewalk, near where I'd been abruptly stopped, and took a step east toward 5th

Avenue, as I had. At that moment, he obviously hit that "glass wall," as well. He tried once more. Boom! He was stopped. Looking perplexed, he turned around, walked back across the blacktop to where I was, on the other side of the street, and we both walked over to 5th Avenue, "unmolested." I was not alone in that "intervention."

That happened to me one other time. Sandy and I were near our vacation property on Puget Sound, taking a walk through the woods. I hit that glass wall again, though, this time, it didn't feel like a physical barrier. I looked around. There were a few forest service men working nearby on some trees, on a tree farm. There was no one looking at us. I quietly told Sandy to turn around, walk, don't run, to the road we had left, and don't ask questions. I saw no threatening actions or "looks" from the men off in the woods, who were legitimately working there. But what I experienced was every bit as invisibly confronting and insistent, as my Manhattan experience. We returned to that forest road and continued back to our lake cabin without further incident. As far as I'm concerned, it was one more divine intervention in my life, just as others had been. I don't know why or how, in each case. But I have no doubt that it was of the Lord, and I'm eternally grateful.

Now back to Utah: A sense of humor was necessary, as an example, because of the "left-handed" compliments that came at us with regularity, in one form or another. Our daughter Linda would be told by her fellow students, "*You're such a good person that you surely must be a Mormon.*" I would get the same type of "compliment" when I'd speak well at a public funeral or memorial service, or some other public gathering, and someone would come up to me at the end of the service to compliment me, and say, *"That was such a good talk, I thought for sure that you were a (Mormon) bishop."* The inference left unsaid was, no one that good, or that well spoken, could be anything but a Mormon. We Gentiles would smile warmly, and move on.

A series of events caused me to lose my sense of humor, and thus, my effectiveness in ministry, which required me to conclude my pastoral service in that culture. Each event said to me, you don't, and you won't ever, belong here. The first event could have been weathered, had it stood alone. A popular Salt Lake City radio station manager, knew of some of my former radio work, and approached me about putting together a 60 second devotional thought each weekday morning, following the five minute NBC radio "news on the hour" drive-time. I said, *"Yes, I'd be glad to give it a try."* It became quite popular. Next, this manager said to me that the Mormon Tabernacle Choir produces excellent music, but it is all of one genre. There are so many excellent varieties of Christian music that are never heard in the Salt Lake Valley, because the only music produced by the Mormon Church is the Mormon Tabernacle Choir. So he wondered if I could put together a half hour Christian music radio program on this "Easy Listening" radio station, on Sunday mornings. I agreed to give this opportunity a try, as well. It would be a bit tricky to present the Christian gospel message to a largely Mormon audience, while not offending their religious/cultural sensitivities.

I did more than just tape a half hour of music, each Sunday morning. I developed a different theme, each week. I'd do a bit of devotional and reflective talking, then play music that supported the theme, then share another thought or two, supported by more music on the theme. This program was broadcast throughout Utah, western Wyoming, and southern Idaho. According to the program audience rating service, it became the most popular Sunday morning radio program in those three states. That was enough to get the station owner to take me off the air, both for the drive time devotion, and the Sunday morning program. When I went in to do my taping, the program manager said to me, "*Didn't they tell you? You're off the air.*"

No, they hadn't told me. I went to the station owner to confirm that I was out of a job. He assured me that the news was true. I reminded him that the ratings folks say that mine was the number one program in a three state region. (Admittedly, Sunday morning radio audiences did not constitute huge numbers of listeners.) He acknowledged that that was correct. "*Okay, just so that we understand each other, I'm being taken off the air because I'm too popular. Right?*"

"*That's right,*" he said. He was not willing to support a Christian pastor becoming so popular on his radio station. Boosting his ratings did not trump his determination to block any perceived competition with the Church Of Jesus Christ Of Latter Day Saints.

In 1984, a major build up of winter snow in the Wasatch Mountains, on the eastern edge of Salt Lake City, Bountiful, and Ogden, caused some serious flooding in the springtime. City engineers in SLC were ingenious in creating a couple of artificial riverbeds through downtown business district. They gave a call to the citizens of the community to help fill sandbags at a warehouse. These sandbags were then trucked out onto State Street.

The plan was to artificially block the major creek at the north end of the business district, near Temple Square, kicking the water up onto State Street, which was turned into a riverbed with the sandbags lining each side of the street. The water then flowed down to Sixth South, where it joined an artificial channel coming from the Wasatch on that street that had intercepted a second major creek. The combined floodwaters could then flow westward out to the Great Salt Lake, without doing any flood damage to the city. It worked beautifully.

Our high school son Mike and I joined the effort by filling, and tossing onto the trucks, about two thousand pounds of sandbags. Other Baptists worked on the lines, helping to create the channels, while the kitchen crew at the church made three thousand sandwiches and prepared drinks for the workers on the lines. After the crisis was over, First Baptist Church received a certificate from the mayor for all the work we did to help save the city. There was a lot of press coverage for the national news services, showing how many different groups of folks helped to save Salt Lake City and the environs.

In 1985, we were destined to experience a repeat performance of the springtime floods. This time we'd be even better prepared than we had been in 1984. I notified city hall that the folks of First Baptist Church would be ready to prepare sandwiches and drinks again, for the line workers. Our members also tried to volunteer for the various physical labor jobs. However, we were informed that the only way that we could participate was to join a Mormon Ward in our various neighborhoods. Only those identifying as Mormons would be allowed to help in saving the city. Somehow, that was not our city, those were not our homes too, and our help in rescuing our neighbors' homes and businesses from disaster was not welcome, if we insisted on working as Christians, rather than as Mormons.

In Bountiful, which was the first bedroom community just north of Salt Lake City, they did not build channels to manage the flood. But they did put sensors into the dirt at the top of the two canyons, where the water would rush down at tremendous force, if those natural barriers gave way. If there was any earth movement, the sensors sent an alarm to the people, who would then have about ten minutes to evacuate the city, when the floodwaters broke through and started rushing down those canyons. But who would receive that alarm? Not the whole citizenry. The alarm would notify the Mormon Ward houses; and Ward volunteers would notify their people. The only way that non-Mormons would know of the danger was if they looked out their windows and saw their Mormon neighbors rushing out of their houses to safety. So here were two more evidences that we didn't belong; and in this case, that not even our safety, as part of the community, was of any value.

About the same time as those events came the final straw. I'd had a good relationship with Mormons for close to sixteen years. We agreed to disagree on religious issues, then moved on from there. I'd accepted their many invitations to speak to their groups in an atmosphere of tolerance and respect. So I suspected nothing amiss when I was invited to the University of Utah to speak to a group, in an informal debate format, on the issue of why The Church of Jesus Christ Of Latter Day Saints was not Christian. I readily admit that my presentation material was not an expression of my finest hour. (After it was over, it was more clear to me how I should have presented my side of the debate.) Nevertheless, the essential material was all included, and I held steadfast to my constant rule of interaction, which was that my purpose was never to attack people or The Church, but rather to say, *"This is what the Christian Faith understands the nature of God and Jesus Christ to be; and this is what it takes to be a Christian."*

That event took place in the late morning. By early afternoon, I was being attacked and mocked on several media outlets. At some points, the radio show hosts on talk radio were warning their call-in listeners to tone down what they were saying about me, because their statements were libelous and they could be sued for slander. That was the end of the line for me. I had been betrayed, and my trust was broken. My sense of openness and humor were gone. It would soon be the month of June, and Sandy and I would be heading for Portland, Oregon, to join in celebrating the Biennial of the American Baptist Churches. It was there that we met with members of the Eastwood Baptist Church pulpit committee, who were approaching me a year later, for the second time. Within a couple of months, our house was sold, our family was packed up, and we were heading west out of Salt Lake City, bound for Medford, Oregon.

20

A Different Set of Dynamics

BY EVERY MEASURE, Eastwood was my greatest challenge. In all the other churches I served, something else was the issue. I could address it objectively as something we could all stand back and examine together. At Eastwood, I was the issue; or more precisely, my simple presence as the pastor, along with my skills, were the issue. When my predecessor left, a hundred plus members left the church with him; and when I arrived, another hundred plus members left. For some, I wasn't their beloved former pastor; so it didn't matter who I was or what I had to offer. For others, I'm not who they wanted after all.

The Search Committee was instructed to hire someone who was more intellectual in the presentation of the Gospel than the last pastor. That's who they found in me. *"Well, yes, but that's not what we wanted, after all. We liked all the emotion of the pastor's crying, because being more emotional means being more spiritual. How can we feel the Spirit if we're not emotional?"* That was the attitude of many members of the congregation. I didn't have a base of support in this new church for who I was as a person and a pastor. There was a lot of distrust in the closing months between the pastor and the church leadership before his departure. By the time I was employed, a year later, the resentments were still entrenched in the congregation.

About a month after I arrived, a major church memorial service was planned for one of the "church pillars." His wife called my predecessor and asked him to come back and lead the service. She didn't ask me first, which is the normal protocol. But many were excited that their beloved former pastor was coming back. I was invited to give the pastoral prayer in that service, followed by the visiting pastor's sermon. After the service, I was told that I should step back to associate pastor so that he could return as Senior Pastor. It was conceded that I do give good prayers, but he preaches such wonderful sermons. I was invited to leave on several occasions in those opening months, so that their former pastor would return to Eastwood. One Sunday, I was told that I had the obligation to buy the former pastor's house because he couldn't sell it, and now he's saddled with two mortgages that he cannot afford to pay. The fact that I had already purchased a home made no difference.

Another peculiar thing is that the congregation loved to play off the clergy staff against one another. The more estranged the pastoral staff was from each other, the greater the pleasure in the minds of several in the congregation. That tactic had worked well with my predecessors. After we hired Michael Sayler as my associate, Sandy and I and he and Margie went on a vacation together. We toured up through northern Oregon and Washington. We stayed a night at our vacation "cabin" on Puget Sound, explored the territory around Mt. Rainier, went up to see the remains of Mt. St.

Helens. We came back the best of friends – all four of us. Many church members were truly upset. They were hoping that our close living together for a week would have us fighting with each other by the time we got back home. With glee in their eyes, they'd actually ask Mike or me, *"Are you still friends?"* – hoping, of course, that the answer was, *"No."* They acted a bit crestfallen when we talked of our strengthened friendships.

This was the first congregation I served as pastor, where I received anonymous "hate mail." One of the letters was sadly humorous. Her criticism was that I was not a loving pastor because I never revealed my inner self to the congregation. If I really cared about people, I'd reveal my inner thoughts and secrets to the congregation from the pulpit. Then she closed with the statement that she would not sign this letter because she didn't trust me. Hmmm . . . But I should trust her with my deepest secrets? How can this be a truly Christian community that honors a loving God?

There was another adjustment with which I had to deal. Admittedly, though I consider myself theologically an Evangelical Christian, I didn't blend well with the Evangelical community that was in southern Oregon, those Evangelicals in Eastwood, or those in the greater Rogue Valley community. In Salt Lake City, at one point I was president of both the Ecumenical Ministerial Association and the Evangelical Ministerial Association at the same time. I could get along well with folks on both sides of the aisle. But in Medford, I could not embrace the negative, sometimes spiteful, unChrist-like spiritual attitude that I found in the Evangelical community, and in the church. One of our evangelical young husbands in the church was quite upset with me, week after week. One day, he came up with the excuse he needed. He told me that I didn't always announce that I was going to pray. Sometimes, in the service, or a meeting, I'd talk to the people and then I'd bow my head and pray (talk) to God. Since I didn't always announce when I was going to pray, he didn't know when to close his eyes. So he was taking his family out of Eastwood, and they'd find a church where he'd know when the prayer was coming so that he could close his eyes at the right time.

Our Children's Minister worked part time in a store in the shopping Mall. One of her fellow employees was the wife of a minister of a small Evangelical church. Her income from that store was essential to their financial survival. One day, she cashed her paycheck. (As I recall, it was about $500, which was a good amount of money at that time.) She put the cash in her purse and put her purse under the counter. Apparently, someone saw her do that, and when she was on the other side of the store he reached over the counter and stole the purse with her payday money inside. She was beside herself. What were she and her husband going to do?

Our person working there told me about what happened and asked if we could help. I told her that we were having an Evangelical Ministers' Council lunch. I'd see what I could do. At the right time, I told them the story, and told them that I thought our churches should chip in to cover the loss. The leader of the group called us to pray for the family. After the "amen," he went on to other business. I interrupted: *"Excuse me, but what are we going to do about this pastoral family that's in trouble?"*

He responded that we'd given the problem to the Lord;

it's no longer our responsibility; God will take care of it. The others in attendance agreed. That was the last time I ever attended an Evangelical Ministers' Council meeting. I went back to my office, got the Deacons to okay the contribution, and Eastwood covered that pastoral couple's loss. Actually, I guess that Evangelical leader was right. The Lord did take care of it. Eastwood was His agent of compassion.

In the end, I couldn't be what my detractors wanted me to be. I could only be who and what I am, and do what I do best. At that point, we began to build a ministry that lasted for eighteen years. As early as the 1960's, when we moved into our new church home in Seattle, I experimented with a variety of ways to worship. One was to worship in the round, centering the entire worship service on the celebration of communion as I continually moved around to address all of the people during the service. Another, given that it was the 1960's, was to develop a folk mass, from time to time, in our worship repertoire. When I became pastor at Eastwood, in Medford, in the 1980's, I attended regional denominational meetings; conferences and gatherings where I began hearing more and more praise music, mostly of the Gaither style in those days. Our congregation loved the old hymns. So did I. But I felt that I needed to introduce our people to some of the types of music that other Christians were singing. At the same time, I wanted to do it in a way that would not send traditional folks running for the exits. So every other week, at first, I began putting together medleys of praise songs and hymns for the worship services. It took a lot of work because I wanted all of the music to be in the same key, for each medley, with words that fit a theme so that the music would blend smoothly into each piece and flow back again – maybe singing a couple verses of a hymn, flow into a complementary praise song, and move back into the chorus of the hymn to close. Early on, I might introduce the medley with a devotional thought centered on what we'd be singing. Within a couple of years, our people were regularly singing from a repertoire of over a hundred fifty songs and hymns.

Before the era of computers and Power Point, I began introducing slides and VHS tapes to enhance our worship as well. If the opening of the worship service was to be the praise of God, I'd get some NASA slides of space – the planets, stars, and galaxies – to cause a sense of wonder and awe among the worshippers. Maybe the theme would be on faith, and I'd show a video of a kayaker going down the Colorado River rapids through the Grand Canyon, leading up to a time of prayer for the perilous and challenging times we're living in. Perhaps I'd show a short video featuring the rising sun casting its rays on a mountain peak, as we pick up the theme by singing "Morning Has Broken," or "When Morning Gilds The Skies." One Sunday, my sermon subject was focused on the message of Michelangelo's "Pieta." I had taken slides of the "Pieta" when I was in Rome, so I had the sound guy show those slides, at the right moment in the sermon. (Though I complain about the use/abuse of screen visuals in worship today, I must own up to being one of the early-day users of that medium of communication.)

We developed some healthy children's and youth programs, and began attracting new folks to the church and to the gospel, that helped to replace some of the folks who had left us. We'd never be a huge church; but we'd be a family where everyone's important and everyone has an opportunity to share in ministry. And we'd all know that we are part of the "Family of God," which became our theme. As Carolyn Dusenberry put it, *"I love the feeling of being a part of a church family. At Eastwood everyone really cares about you."*

We were also entering an era of social and moral/ethical upheaval. Christendom in the western world was collapsing. "Christendom" doesn't mean that the whole population accepts the Christian Faith, and that every citizen has committed her/his life to God through Christ. It means that generally speaking, the populations of western nations accept the existence of the Biblical God, and the moral/ethical guidelines of the Ten Commandments as the universal model of the land for what is right and wrong. And it provided an Ultimate Authority in the will of God, to which the vast majority of people adhered. Two incidents demonstrated that for me. The first was when we arrived in Hay and found out that the entire community wanted to vote favorably on me coming to be the pastor of the church even though many were not members of that church. The community was afraid that that little church might have to close its doors. They didn't plan on attending worship on Sunday mornings, but they wanted it there as a moral influence in their community.

The second illustration of Christendom for me came when Sandy and I visited the Police museum in Balboa Park in San Diego. There was an old 1920's Paddy Wagon on display that had no door on the back, where those who would be transported to jail, were held. I asked why there was no door. The guide's explanation was that in those days, everyone knew what was right and what was wrong. Some folks planned on doing the wrong thing, like stealing or attacking someone; but they also knew it was wrong, and if you were caught, you were caught and paid the price. So the suspect needed no door. If he was arrested, he stayed put. In these days, there is no such common mental attitude. Authority is not to be obeyed, particularly if you can break free of it. So in these days, every police car is a traveling mini-jail, with bars, locked doors, shackle rings, etc.

Following the social revolution of the 1960's-70's, which featured such things as "free love," rejection of ultimate authority, many folks played with his/her own god/goddess of the month. Commonly accepted morality and ethics disappeared. With the loss of the authority of scripture, long-held traditional interpretations of human deportment went by the wayside along with commonly accepted universal truths. This was a mixed bag of benefits and curses. We were finally beginning to address the issue of the equality of women as more than just theory, which was a good thing. While still in Salt Lake City, I became intentional about looking for young women with leadership potential. I encouraged them to no longer just stand over by the wall getting the coffee and cookies ready for the board meeting, or taking the minutes. Instead, I encouraged some to make themselves available, and accept a position on the governing board. By the time I left that church, we had a woman Moderator. I encouraged them, in the business world, as well, to believe in themselves and strive for higher positions in the company than were typically available to them.

At the same time that new freedoms of opportunity were developing, as moves were being made toward gender equality, traditional morality was collapsing. For example, young couples who most often attended the new praise churches, started coming to me as they struggled with the traditional moral stance of the Church, which was chastity before marriage. But they lived in a secular society that was openly inviting a new generation into what we used to call "pre-marital sex." Reinforcing the concept of "free love," one of the current Broadway musicals declared, in song, that casual sex is *the friendliest thing two people can do.*" It was a time when "fifteen minute couples" having sex, didn't want to know each other's names. That would make it too personal and suggest some kind of commitment. The young adults visiting me for counseling on this issue were deciding that although genital to genital sex may still be morally wrong before marriage, how about oral sex? Would oral sex be okay? They were looking for me to give them a free pass so that they could enjoy sex without marriage and still be good Christians.

"Living together" was becoming as popular as marriage. Was that long-term fornication? To this day, I wonder if I did the right thing, when I delayed indefinitely the baptism of a young woman in our church who was living with a man who was abusing her and her child. I told her she should wait until she either married the man or left him. (I was hoping she would leave him, and I told her so.) She did neither. She stayed in the church and served where she could. My rationale at the time was that she was living in sin; and to continue to live in that state, after giving her life to Christ and being baptized with Him into salvation, made it a commitment without a change in life; and I couldn't promote that. On the one hand, a "piece of paper" does not make a lifetime commitment. On the other hand, if you want a marriage arrangement without the marriage, then the question is,

"What is it that keeps you from making a lifetime commitment?" The reality is that the qualities of both commitment and loyalty were beginning to crumble in all segments of society.

Homosexuality is another issue that is tearing the Church Universal apart, and it's a problem for me. I'm deeply conflicted. At one point I must declare, unequivocally, that every human being is made in the image of God and must be honored as such. A second point is the Bible makes strong statements against the "gay lifestyle." And the third point is that I accept that the gay life is not simply a choice for the majority of gay people, but rather, is an innate part of who that person is. That being the case, I cannot imagine how a person can be morally judged for accepting who she/he innately is. I do believe that there is no room in the Christian Faith for promiscuity in either the heterosexual or gay life. We have had gay people of both genders participating in the life of every church I've served, except for the first one. This includes one person who struggled with being HIV positive as a result of her husband's sexual activities. I've also worked to support a woman in the congregation who was the mother of a son slowly dying of AIDS. It's a pain she shares with almost no one. Going back to my essential choice which I made in Seattle, I am the pastor to all of the people in my congregation; and I will serve each one with as much support and guidance as I know how to give, regardless of their sins or circumstances, hopes, fears and dreams. My guiding scripture is found in Galatians 3:28: *"There is neither Jew nor Greek, slave nor free, male nor female, for you are all one in Christ Jesus."* In that spirit, I am called to be faithful to the flock for whom I am a shepherd; and the Lord will sort it all out according to His great compassionate and loving will.

Meanwhile, we stayed creative with ministry, experimenting with a Saturday evening worship in the Fellowship Hall while sitting around tables with light refreshments available. Our Associate Pastor led those services until he accepted a call to be a senior pastor of a church in California. We also worked on a drop-in center for Middle School kids after school was out, for kids walking passed our church on the way home. Block parties for the community were another event we tried. Some forms of outreach worked, some, not so much. Thanksgiving food boxes to the hungry in our community was a big project every November.

We also began a ministry with teen parents at North Medford High School. That school provided educations for youth who were active parents. Some had no support from their families. A couple of them lived in their cars. There was daycare for the babies while moms, and occasionally, a dad, attended classes. Some of our folks went weekly to the school to help out. We brought them all to the church at Christmas for a big Christmas party where we sang Christmas carols, told the true Christmas story, fussed over their kids, and gave them all Christmas presents. Most of those parents had never received such love before. Then, during the week of Mother's Day, we held a big celebration again, expressing the love of Jesus for them through our own kindnesses. As Glenda, one of the Eastwood Family's members put it in a church publication, *"Eastwood has a unique combination of a warm caring family atmosphere and the stimulation of challenging Biblical teaching. The people really live out their Christian commitment"* (Glenda Cossette).

21

The Traveling Christians

I HAD BEEN A COUNSELOR for about forty years when I retired. At one point, after we had moved to Medford, while my counseling ministry continued to grow, I was invited to become a Diplomate, then a Life Diplomate, of the American Psychotherapy Association. I helped to design a couple of chaplaincy qualification programs for the Association.

In that same time frame, 1988, I was invited to be part of a team of about twenty psychiatrists, psychologists and counselors to travel to the Soviet Union, representing the United States, to compare counseling techniques in the two different cultures and political structures.

For me, traveling to the Soviet Union was a life-affecting experience. What frustrated me greatly was that Sandy could not be with me and share in my experiences in Russia and Uzbekistan. I had very few photos to show because it was not wise to shoot lots of photos in a Communist country. Often, we were told to put away our cameras, by our ever-present guides. So I could not help Sandy feel and see what I'd felt and seen. I vowed that I'd never take another trip overseas, without her.

Wouldn't you know that irony would soon bite me? I was invited, by a Masonic group to participate in an all expense paid trip to the Holy Land for clergy. It was a wonderful opportunity. But wives were not invited. *"I won't go!"* I said. I wasn't going overseas again without Sandy.

Her response was, *"Don't be a fool!"*

So again, I had a life-affecting adventure overseas that made a significant difference in my preaching and Bible studies of which Sandy was not a part. But this time I figured out a solution: I'll organize tours myself. That way, Sandy can go with me. I organized two different tours to Israel, plus parts of the Palestinian Territories, after my own journey there. The second Israel tour included an optional tour of Jordan, which dramatically affected the lives of many of the folks of Eastwood. Over the life of those tours, close to a hundred members of our Eastwood Family went on at least one tour; a bunch of them went on all of the tours. This greatly strengthened the fellowship in the congregation. I developed a tour that followed "The Footsteps of Paul" through Turkey and Greece. It was so satisfying when I could refer to places we had seen, and the dozens of folks from the church who made at least one of those trips, could call up images in their minds of Biblical places we had been together.

The spirit of friendship continued to grow throughout the congregation when we joined a work tour in the Czech Republic shortly after the fall of the Soviet Empire. There, we helped a small Baptist congregation convert a three hundred year old city hall into a prayer house. (The Czech Christians don't refer to their places of worship as churches. For them, the people are the church; and the church comes together on Sundays to worship in a prayer house.) The women took on the scaffold work of scraping the plaster off the ceiling of the worship hall, about thirty feet up. We men ripped three hundred year old straw insulation out of other ceilings, built new ceilings, and re-plastered the walls. There was a fair amount of carpentry and electrical work to be accomplished as well.

Our women also taught the Czech women how to do children's ministry. In Communist nations, all Christians had "Christian" stamped on their passports. Under Communism, Christians weren't allowed to have anything to do with children other than their own. That meant that they could not be schoolteachers, work for the welfare department, or in medical clinics where they would come into contact with children. Though they could have Sunday school for their own children, they could not reach out to the kids in the community. So our women used part of their workday to develop a sort of Vacation Bible School type program for the kids in the public housing project across the boulevard from the prayer house. The program included lots of singing, circle running games, Bible stories, etc. guiding the Czech women in the process. It caught on amazingly well. Before long, the kids were crossing the street to wait outside the prayer house for our women to hurry up and come across the street for more singing, playing, and storytelling, out on the lawn of the housing project.

After our work project was finished, we took a tour up into Poland and visited the site of Schindler's Factory in Krakow. Then we went on to have our hearts broken by visiting nearby Auschwitz and Birkenau death camps. We then continued on through Slovakia, to Budapest and

Hungary, before returning home. One final tour took us to Western Europe, beginning in Brussels and ending in Rome, and the Coliseum, where so many Christians died for their faith in the early days of the church. I was surprised at how emotional I became in the Coliseum when I looked down and pictured the Christians being slaughtered for their faith. I shed some tears. This was a final cap for our Biblical and missionary journeys, and secured a rich heritage for the Faith in the lives of many in the Eastwood family.

As I moved toward the latter years of my ministry, our daughter, Linda Tripp, became leader of the praise band in the worship service, which added a new and complementary dimension to our organ music. Her husband, Andy, became the sound and video person for the services. She became more and more involved in the worship services. After I retired, she stayed on. When the organist retired, Linda became the piano accompanist for the whole service. For a time, she also held the position of worship director. Before my retirement, Linda was her father's daughter. It didn't take long after my retirement for me to become my daughter's father. I'm very proud of that. Fifteen years later, her participation in worship, and her teaching in a Christian elementary school, are still the focus points of her ministry.

On the occasion of the fortieth anniversary of my ordination, the Eastwood Family planned a surprise celebration of the occasion. Everyone in the church knew that it was coming except me. I found that many lies were told from the pulpit that were accurately interpreted by everyone in the know while I remained ignorant of all that was going on around me, as they planned for the surprise. The bogus gathering that I heard them planning had little interest to me, and Sandy had to nearly drag me to that Saturday afternoon event. I was totally caught off guard when I walked into the fellowship hall to be greeted by some members of my former churches, as well as a room filled with well-wishers from Eastwood. They outdid themselves in their planning for the event that was to honor me. I was close to being speechless at this outpouring of love.

A year later, when I announced my retirement, I knew that they would plan another celebration in my honor. So I found out who was in charge of the planning. I knew that the women's group was planning a reception for Sandy, so I asked her not to honor me. That was beautifully done a year earlier. I asked them, instead, to expand the women's event to honor Sandy into a full-blown celebration and allow the whole church to honor their pastor's wife. What a marvelous job they did, recognizing all of the contributions she had made and the ministries she had performed for that congregation and the greater community over the past eighteen years. I could not have been more pleased and gratified to see her be so richly honored. That was a gift beyond price, and a fitting conclusion to our ministry at that point.

22

Fashion Magazines, a Frisbee, Sam and Ivan, and McDonalds

THIS WHOLE CHAPTER is **an aside** in that it's a reflection on how I was affected by my tour of the USSR. In Moscow, we American counselors and psychiatrists met with our Russian counterparts at a sex clinic where we talked mostly about alcoholism. It turned out that they had a much better handle on dealing with that addiction than we did. Alcoholism was the number one physical and mental health problem in that nation. They not only dealt with the victim of addiction, but they also had the authority to go into his/her workplace to see what working conditions prevailed where he/she works, and determine what adjustments could be made to reduce the stress on the client. Then they went to the family home to study the dynamics of their client's family life and consider ways to reduce the stress issues in the family. At this point, we Americans were envious of our Soviet counterparts' freedom to do such extensive work, gaining a much greater understanding of their patients' overall lives, as they worked on programs of recovery.

In the Islamic culture of Central Asia, we spent time in the cities of Samarkand, Bukhara, and Tashkent. We were there just as the Russian armies where pulling out of Afghanistan. As we took a side trip down to Dushanbe, Tadzhikistan, right above the Afghanistan border, we were confronted with seemingly endless troop trucks filled with Russian soldiers, interspersed with heavy artillery, tanks on flatbeds, etc., all returning to the Homeland, after ending the failed occupation of that nation to the south.

In the Muslim communities, we found very little in the way of effective, or even existing, counseling services. Sadder still, what was offered had almost nothing to offer women who lived under deplorable social restrictions. In one clinic, we listened to a husband and father tell us about his wife. She was a well-known ballerina in that region of the world, receiving a number of awards and accolades for her artistry in dance. But then, she must come home, prepare the meal for her husband and children in their tiny, ill-equipped, apartment. After they ate their meals, she could eat hers – and then, wash the dishes in the bathtub, since they had no kitchen sink. He had a sense that there was something wrong with that picture; and he had some sympathy for her position. But he said that that's the norm in their culture, and he was not sure just how he could fix it to remove some of the stress in his wife's life. They had a long way to go, but I found a sense of hope in that he was willing to define a specific problem and wonder, within the context of his culture, how the problem might be lessened to the benefit of his wife whom he seemed to genuinely love.

On our rather long bus ride from Samarkand to Bukhara,

I concluded that maybe I had too casually offered my opinions on healthcare providers and their inability to work well with death and dying patients. The result was, I suddenly had an assignment during that bus ride. I had about five minutes to prepare a twenty minute lecture to deliver to the group from the front of the bus, using the driver's microphone, while standing and riding backwards in a vehicle that was hitting every bump and pavement groove on that poor highway. My impromptu topic was, "Death Is A Failure Experience," as far as the health care community is concerned. My thesis was that, with the assumption that death is a failure experience for healthcare providers, from nurses to therapists, to doctors, they are rendered powerless to deal with critical issues of life. They are so uncomfortable with the death issue that they essentially abandon these patients during the dying process. Apparently I did well, for I got a number of compliments. And as an added bonus, I did not get motion sickness once during that rough and tumble backwards ride.

Up in Leningrad (now St. Petersburg), we Americans found some humor in our time spent with psychiatrists in a mental hospital. Communist mental hospitals were notorious around the world as "prisons," where unwilling "patients" were assigned by the courts as a form of political punishment. But apparently, there was some real psychiatric treatment going on in those hospitals as well.

Glasnost (openness) and *Perestroika* (reform), associated with Communist Dictator Mikhail Gorbachev, were well underway when we were there. The Soviet Union was beginning to crumble. One of the effects of that was that patients could no longer be held against their will in mental hospitals. The biggest question that the Soviet psychiatrists had for their American counterparts was, *"How can you get your psychiatric work done when the patient doesn't have to remain in the hospital?"* That, of course, is an ongoing question for American counselors all of the time, at all levels of therapy. That was a fun exchange, which forced us to go back and review our own methods of engagement to see what does, and does not, work in engaging clients at a level where they will see the value of the work we are doing together. Another fallout of that moment in history was that a number of Soviet leaders wanted to meet with us Americans to pick our brains about our way of life under democracy and capitalism. The greatest shocker to me was that we were told that they had sent some young Soviet economists to Georgetown University to learn about capitalist economics – its strengths and pitfalls. One more surprise: When I got home I told people that they could expect to see the collapse of the Soviet Union within a couple of years. Some of our folks here at home actually got mad at me for saying that. One couple even left the church. Sometimes we need to have an enemy in place in order to define our own lives, by knowing who we are not, and "knowing" why we are superior to them. So when we lose that enemy, we lose an important part of our identities as humans.

I was a child during World War II, and very much aware of the war effort. Living in Portland, Oregon, we were subject to the air raid wardens patrolling our streets at night, making sure that our black window shades were pulled down, our bathtubs were full of water as a resource in case our water systems were destroyed or contaminated; and, of course, there were the air raid drills at school. Living on a bluff overlooking the

Willamette River and the Union Pacific rail yards, I saw the warships being built, and those already commissioned docked in our safe harbor. I went to sleep every night, with arc welder flashes lighting up the Portland clouds and my darkened bedroom. Every night it was like living through a great lightning storm, coming from the 24-hour-a-day construction of one warship after another in the shipyards below. I saw the many troop trains full of soldiers and sailors being brought by rail from the Midwest and East, ready to embark on troop ships. The flatbed cars of the trains were filled with newly made cannons, jeeps, half-tracks and tanks, all ready to be shipped overseas, and all passing below our house. Along with the food, rubber tire, and gasoline rationing, we kids had to regularly take our wagons around our neighborhoods on paper drives and tin can drives, collecting them all for the war effort. There just was no way to avoid being completely involved in the whole world-at-war mentality. When I was old enough, my Grandpa Haynes told me more than once, *"After we defeat Germany, Russia will be our next enemy."* He barely lived to see it; but it turns out that he was right.

Next, I lived as a teenager and young adult through the Cold War, and because of that I developed the typical prejudices against Communism. Joseph McCarthy was creating havoc in political America in the late 1940's. Meanwhile, Congressman Jelke was taking his House Un-American Activities Committee out on the road, traveling all around the country *"Red baiting"* and looking for *"Commie pinkoes"* under every rock. Neighbors turned on each other in Portland, when the Committee came, looking for supposed Communist sympathizers, particularly among the educators. A nearby neighbor had red paint thrown on his house, and his front walk painted yellow. The instant hatred was so fierce that he and his family had to flee out of the city for their safety. They were never proved guilty of anything. It wasn't necessary. The desire to blame others for all our woes never needs the light of truth to show them the way. These victims of the Jelke Committee were accused by workers for a congressional committee, and that was plenty enough evidence for their neighbors to try to destroy them.

Following all of this in America, John Foster Dulles became the much-travelled Secretary of State, who charted a course of "Brinksmanship," under President Eisenhower, (constantly living on the brink of war, in a dozen different places around the globe). That was at the time of the Korean Conflict, where American troops fought the Communist North Koreans and then the Chinese Communist Army of Mao Zedong. All of this is to say that I was well schooled in the evils of Communism and the dangers of the enemy lurking in the Union of Soviet Socialist Republics

Now, it's 1988, and I'm about to land in Moscow on an Aeroflot plane out of Ireland. I'm at a much different mental level. Still, I have some vestiges lurking around my interior, growing out of all of those prejudices from the Cold War era. First of all, when we were in Samarkand, which was a Muslim holy city, I pondered the irony that if we Christians did not have the protection of the Communist presence in Samarkand we could be executed by the Muslims for desecrating their holy city by our presence. Beyond that, four personal experiences lifted me out of my institutional prejudices, which most certainly qualify as **another learning**. The first came when I met our local Intourist guide in

Bukhara. He was a Communist, and an Islamic citizen of Uzbekistan. He had an engaging personality and we quickly connected. His son was an active member of their equivalent of the Boy Scouts. We saw him marching in a parade. His teenage daughter was growing into a young woman. And Muslim or not, she was wanting to try out some new forms of independence, some differing clothing fashions, some new activities, just like girls everywhere across the West want to do. He was a loving Dad who wanted to grant as much to his daughter as possible while protecting her from all manner of troubles that she could create for herself in that heavily restricted society. Somehow he chose me as a safe and understanding person in whom he could confide. There was little I could do but listen, which was likely the most important thing of all. Currently, fashionable clothing was most important to his teenager. So he asked me if I could send him a couple of American fashion magazines featuring teenage clothing styles that he could give to his daughter, that did not feature mostly risqué clothing but would give her some ideas to dream about, and . . . to show that her Dad cared about her interests. I took his address and told him that I'd do it, if at all possible. Back home, I found that U.S. Post Offices could not mail magazines to that part of the world. When I wrote to tell him that I could not send the magazines, I tried to be as careful as I knew how to be, with my wordings, in case the letter was intercepted before he received it from a foreigner.

A couple of days later, we were in Tashkent. We were wandering through a park like area that featured several war memorials. I wandered away from the group and a boy, about 13 or 14, threw me his Frisbee. I threw it back, and we began a game. We never spoke a word to each other. Of course, we couldn't. We just enjoyed each other's company for a time. He was certainly a better player than I was. So after a while, we went our separate ways – another human connection, by way of a Frisbee.

The third event took place in Tashkent, as well. We had some down time at the hotel, so I decided to go for a walk. I walked a couple of blocks off the main thoroughfare, where foreigners were less likely to be. I walked around the corner onto a wide street, and there, in the middle of the block, was a large banner stretching almost curb to curb. On my left was a huge forearm and hand of Uncle Sam, with the red & white striped coat sleeve, and a cuff of blue with white stars, shaking the hand that was coming from the right, also with a forearm, with the Russian symbols on the red sleeve, of Ivan (their equivalent of Uncle Sam). And in English, and in Russian, were the words "Peace." There were not any international negotiations going on. This was not on a thoroughfare that would catch the eye of tourists. This had to be a heartfelt expression of a local peoples' desire to live at peace with their "enemy." I got my camera out and took a photo of it.

Fourth, I asked my Leningrad guide why she became a member of the (Communist) Party. Being an Intourist guide, she had to belong to the Party. Beyond that, she had heart for the downtrodden in their midst. She wanted to help them in their difficulties. The only way that she could do charitable work there was as a Party member. Then she talked about her two teenagers. She wished that they had McDonalds in Russia, like they do in America. Then, her kids could earn their own money and learn a good work ethic. Here was a dad talking to a mom about the plight of the poor people in our midst, and our concern to raise our children to have a good sense of personal responsibility. More, being the same age, we were both kids during WW II. During food rationing, when I didn't want to finish my meal Mom would say, "Finish it. Think of all of the children starving in China." My guide said that the same thing went on in her home in Russia, only her Mom said, "Finish it. think of all the starving children in India." Amazing.

If this was not a learning, it was at least **an awareness upgrade**, that human beings are human beings, regardless of culture, politics, or religion. Whether we were dads being dads, and trying to do the best we can by our kids within the given culture, or playing a pick-up game of Frisbee with a complete stranger in a city park, where language would be a barrier, stumbling onto a banner crying out for Peace with us, or talking with a mom who has a deep passion for helping the poor and downtrodden while she yearns to provide the best possible outcome for her growing teenagers, we shared a common humanity. In spite of the millions of deaths, and immeasurable suffering caused by the Communist government in the gulags and prisons, when we're able to get passed the national politics, we are human souls trying to be as humane as possible, within the political and economic context in which we find ourselves. I travelled to the enemy's homeland. Though I was constantly under the watchful eyes of the KGB, everywhere I went I found a friendly face, along with an outstretched hand in the name of peace. I praise God that I got to see the world, and our heavenly Father's human creatures, a little more clearly, and a smidge closer to the way our Lord sees His human creation, and not as our politics demand that I see them.

23

A Summation and Some Reflections

AND SO, HERE I AM, having served as pastor of five congregations in four states, followed by several engagements as interim pastor at the First Baptist Church of Yreka, California, and Transitional Pastor for Presbyterian churches, the last being First Presbyterian Church of Klamath Falls, Oregon, in 2017, following three stints in various forms of pastoral ministry at Westminster Presbyterian Church in Medford, Oregon, after my first formal retirement from Eastwood Baptist Church of Medford, Oregon, in 2003.

Summary of Experience and Philosophy of Ministry.

Some ministers see their ministry focused on evangelistic preaching and winning souls for Christ, almost exclusively. Some ministers see themselves as politicians, working through political structures to establish and protect traditional Christian values for the nation. Some see themselves as keepers of the ancient liturgies and traditions of the Faith. Others see themselves as Christian social workers feeding the hungry, clothing the naked, housing the homeless, and spurring people on to social action. For most of us, our ministries evolve through time, experience, wisdom gained, and current needs confronting us.

As of this date, I have led 438 funerals and memorial services, officiated at 312 marriages, baptized 352 individuals, and welcomed an additional 539 individuals into church membership.

Out of the 3,629 times that I have preached, there is a sermon which I preached while I served as Transitional Pastor of the Klamath Falls First Presbyterian Church, which seems best to summarize my experience and philosophy of ministry. It reflects that with which I've dealt, what my focus has been, and what my interpretation and emphasis of the Gospel (the Good News), has been, at least through my last two to three decades of ministry. None of my sermons can fully encompass the completeness of my ministerial life. But, at this stage of my life, I think that a sermon entitled "PAIN MEANS LIFE," gets us into the right neighborhood of where I have seen the activity of our loving Lord the most clearly, and where I've been able to most effectively declare the redemptive mercies of our God.

"PAIN MEANS LIFE"

Scripture text: Mark 5:21-34.

In the book *In His Image*, Philip Yancey relates the story of Dr. Paul Brand, a Christian missionary doctor in India, who focused on learning to treat the scourge of leprosy. This interest came to him as he watched a man in New Guinea reaching into a bed of hot coals with his bare hand to turn a roasting potato. From that observation, he concluded that all disfigurement from leprosy derives from a single cause: The person with leprosy cannot feel pain. The result was that the old man no longer treated his fingers as something worth preserving as part of self. They no longer were part of self because they felt no pain. Dr. Brand went on to say, "*A healthy body attends to the pain of the weakest part.*" Pain connects us. We'll get back to the social implications of that statement, as well, in a little bit.

Much later in his practice, Dr. Brand worked with a leprosy patient named Sadan, who also became a close, personal friend. Sadan endured countless numbers of hand surgeries to redirect the most useful muscles and tendons to the most useful fingers. This included transferring nerves to those useful digits. Between surgeries and therapies, the process took four years.

Finally, Sadan wanted to go home to Madras to show off his less deformed self to family and friends. With specially designed rocker shoes to protect his feet, he was all set to go. Arriving back home, he was joyfully and fully accepted – and they held a neighborhood party for him. It was a grand and joyous occasion for Sadan – and an exhausting one as well. He rolled out his mat on the floor and fell into a deep sleep, filled with great peace and contentment.

The next morning, when he awoke, he examined himself as he was taught to do, and he recoiled in horror. His wonderfully repaired fingers were bloody, mangled stumps, with telltale drops of blood all around. He knew immediately what it was: A rat had visited him in the night and gnawed at his fingers. The next night, Sadan was determined not to let that happen again. He'd stay awake all night to protect himself. But he fell asleep while reading by a kerosene lamp. In the morning, he found that the back of his hand had fallen against the lamp and was badly burned. Broken hearted, Sadan returned to the hospital in Vellore. As he poured out his misery to Dr. Brand, he said, "*I feel like I've lost all of my freedom.*" And then he asked: "*How can I be free without pain?*"

Wow!! What a question! What a strange concept to those who have lived with pain, that we should need pain to be free. We're more likely to ask, "*How can I be free with this pain?*"

Dealing with our quadriplegic son for thirty years, Sandy and I can make sense out of that despairing question. Being unable to feel pain has some serious, even life-threatening, consequences that accompany that.

Okay, so what about the social implications of that concept? In my role as a CASA, I sat in a courtroom one day, and I heard the testimony of a young man who had devoted most of his thirty years to a life of crime and drug abuse. He was an addict by the time he was twelve years old. More recently, he had become a single parent to a baby girl. In giving testimony, he told of how his baby developed diarrhea, and she was obviously in pain. He said that for the first time in his life, he felt someone else's pain. When he was on drugs, he never felt anyone's pain. But these hours of having to clean up his tiny daughter, several times, had given him a new experience. Feeling his daughter's pain caused him to bond with her – and, for the first time in his life, to love someone. It was feeling another person's pain for the first time in his life that caused him to bond with, and love, his baby girl. And *that* was turning his life around. He now knew that he had to get clean and make something of himself. He had to get a job and provide a safe home for his baby girl who had taught him to love through her pain.

Let's take a look at some of the drama of Mark's gospel. Jesus was focusing on laying the foundation for Himself in both the Jewish and Gentile worlds: As the Messiah, in the Jewish world, and as the Christ, in the Gentile world. Leprosy was everywhere in Jesus' day. Jesus healed a number of lepers, both Samaritan and Jewish. Varying forms of disease and pain knew no ethnic or racial boundaries in that day, anymore than it does in this day.

In the larger context of this story, Jesus had crossed the lake from the Jewish province of Galilee over to the Gentile territory of the Decapolis on the eastern side of the lake. On the way, He had to calm the storm and the waters to keep the disciples' boat from being swamped, which demonstrated that he was the Master, even of the physical elements of the earth. Then He took a totally out-of-control, violent man who was demon possessed, who had been banished to the cemetery, by the towns people, where he'd not harm any more folks. He was basically put in solitary confinement, which doubled that pain, because he was totally ostracized from living with any other human beings. It was there that Jesus healed and restored the man.

Before He left to sail back to the Galilee, Jesus commissioned the cured man as a missionary to his own people who had persecuted him. Out of this man's pain, which led him to the Lord, came redemption and a high and holy purpose for his life. Hear the word of the Lord: "*So, the man started off to visit the Ten Towns* (Decapolis) *of that region and began to proclaim the great things Jesus had done for him; and everyone was amazed at what he told them.*" This "*nobody,*" this "*being,*" who was treated as a wild animal, was drawn out of his pain and set free. Suddenly, he was testifying to the transforming love and healing power of Jesus.

Meanwhile, Jesus no sooner landed back in the Galilee, than He was surrounded by a football sized crowd. Everyone wanted a piece of Jesus; but two people in particular connected with Him. The first was Jairus, a synagogue leader, who met Jesus on the shore and fell at Jesus' feet. You can feel his pain and sense of desperation: His beloved daughter is terminally ill and she's running out of time. There are no medical solutions; Jesus is this Dad's only hope. *"Come quickly! Don't waste a moment. Maybe, if You get their fast enough, Master, You can keep her alive!"*

So Jesus, and that huge crowd, started walking on the highway toward Jairus' home. They're all pushing and shoving and jostling, with all kinds of people trying to get close to Jesus. The disciples were trying to act like bodyguards, to give Jesus some walking space. Poor Jairus, of course, is going crazy. He's trying to get Jesus to move faster. Suddenly, Jesus stopped and asked, "*Who touched me?*"

The disciples asked, "*What, are you nuts?! Everyone is pushing and shoving everyone. What do you mean, 'Who touched me?'*"

"*Somebody touched me,*" Jesus said. That person had touched Him differently than all the others. That person had touched Him in faith, and He had felt power, the power of healing, drain from His body. When the crowd separated, there was a woman who had been suffering from a non-stop menstrual flow for twelve years. Not only was that debilitating physical malady plaguing her, but in that culture, she was considered unclean and could not socialize with anyone. She could not even go to the Temple to worship God. She suffered physically, socially, and spiritually. She went broke paying for useless treatments by the doctors of the day. She was a nobody until this moment: Now, that faceless woman became the only <u>face</u> in that whole faceless crowd.

Jesus responded to her. Her faith in the Messiah had healed her physically. Now, Jesus would complete the job by healing her socially and spiritually. He honored her humanity. He honored her worth as a child of God . . . and then, He continued on His journey to deal with Jairus' little girl, who by now had died. But, because of the faith of her Dad, and maybe because Jesus loves the little children, He entered the girl's bedroom and raised her back to life. So now we have three "nobodies" whom the Christ made "somebodies" – people who were, each one, saved through their pain.

Jesus had released that woman to become a fully human, contributing, creative person, once again. We may have been lost in mental illness, or in a dark cloud of rebellious anger, or in the back rooms of addiction and drunkenness. We suppose that no one will ever care enough to find us. But however badly anyone has messed up, no one can be so lost that even God has lost track of us. That's true whether you're an astronaut on the moon, or a spelunker in the deepest cave on earth. It's true whether you're a ragamuffin kid, struggling to survive, but about to give up, or a sick, non-descript woman in a crowd that's surrounding Jesus. God is there for us in the midst of the pain, waiting for us to let Him embrace us.

We come at this in different ways, meeting different circumstances, peculiar to each of us. In Hosea 11, God the Father cries out, *"My heart is torn within Me, and My compassion overflows,"* as He reached out to His recalcitrant chosen people. God the Son, felt healing power drain from His body, as that poor, outcast, suffering woman reached through the indifferent legs of the crowd to touch the hem of Jesus' robe. His compassionate love reached out to her; it honored her faith and redeemed her more fully than she could ever have dreamed possible.

It's not about these people "deserving" what they got. God's compassion touched them in spite of their rebellion and stubbornness . . . in spite of them being victims of the capricious happenstance of physical disease that attacks some of us and not others. The Lord's love repaired their bodies and souls, though none of them had earned it. Jesus' mercy will surround us and give us hope regardless of what pains and brokenness other peoples' sins have caused to overwhelm us.

As Christians, we are disciples of the Messiah. We're called to the great adventure of reaching out to those in need: the broken, the discouraged, those lost on a path they should not have chosen. If we follow the example of our Savior, reaching out in the name of Christ might be treating a young boy like a valuable human being for the first time in his life. It might be seeing a need in a newly widowed person and performing some menial tasks on her behalf while reminding her of how much God loves her. Or, perhaps it's providing some respite care for a single mom who has just about come to the end of her string. . Maybe it's being the source of hope in Christ, for someone living in the pain of unemployment. For God makes sure that each of us has a purpose, and something helpful and creative that we can do in this world, in the name of Christ our Lord, if we'll just claim it."

End of Sermon.

I don't do well without a purpose for my living that guides me in some form of service. So, in 2005, after batting about for a time in retirement, I went through the three month training regimen and background checks, and was sworn in as an officer of the court, known as a Court Appointed Special Advocate – a CASA, as I described, earlier in this memoir. Each CASA case will take a minimum of a year; most take an average of two years. So far, the longest case I've had lasted six years, and another, four years. Protecting vulnerable children and encouraging, confronting, and supporting both parents and children through the most difficult times of their lives, as we move, in the majority of cases, to a successful recovery takes specialized skills and understanding, patience, and a non-judgmental spirit, all of which I have. At the same time, I hold people firmly to accountability when they do damage to themselves and others. By law, I am to remain neutral to all parties and agencies involved in the case, representing only the child, and his/her best interests. However, I feel that one of the best things I can do for that child is to help them get rehabilitated parents back. So I tell the parent that I will encourage her/him, offer advice and insights, confront her when she's making poor choices, and help her/him to understand the issues. As we go along. I promise that I will never lie to him/her; and I sternly warn her never to lie to me. It will go badly for her if she does. (Those parents never do lie to me.) I also warn them that if they "cross the line," wherever that line is, and we'll both know it, I'll turn on her in a heartbeat to move to protect the child. With tough love, in about 70% of the cases, we have successful returns of rehabilitated children being returned to rehabilitated parents.

In a reflection on what I'm doing at this stage of my life, being part of the county judicial system, I know that I cannot advocate for the Christian Faith and personal commitments to the Savior, which I might do as a pastor.

Still, I have a number of opportunities as an officer of the court that I never had as a pastor. When the occasion calls for it, I'll ask, "*Have you thought about praying for that?*" I need not say anymore. Having access to specific prisoners in the jail is another example. Earlier in this memoir, I related how reminding a prisoner of God's love for her/him, can be transforming. One time, I was contacting a mom who was living in a residential setting. We were talking in a small room, where there was a Bible on a shelf. She pointed to the Bible and said, "*I wish I had a Bible of my own.*" I said nothing; but a few days later, I bought a particular translation of the Bible I wanted her to have. Since I'd be seeing her in court in a couple of hours, I took it with me, carrying it in the store shopping sack. I quietly handed it to her as we sat together waiting to be called up before the judge. She just had to pull that Bible out of the bag and start leafing through it there in the courtroom.

Just then, we were called up before the judge. As we sat down at the table, the judge asked her, "*What have you got there?*"

She responded, "*A Bible. My CASA gave me a Bible as a gift.*"

"*Well,*" said the judge. "*You be sure to spend a lot of time reading that Bible.*"

As we proceeded on with the status of this mom's case for the day, I thought to myself, "*When, as a pastor, would I ever have had the opportunity to introduce a Bible into a court of law and have all present hear the judge advise the client to read her new Bible?*"

24

From Pastor to Badass

PEOPLE ASK ME what it's like to be a CASA. My typical response is, *"It is the most frustrating, heartbreaking job you'll ever love."* My very first case fell into that category. The mother was a sexual abuser of her four-year-old daughter and six-year-old son. It was ongoing. The daughter expressed to me how much mommy hurt her, and hurt her brother, through sexual molestation. We moved them to foster care. Fortunately, I found some relatives in another state that turned out to be ideal folks to care for these children. We were finally able to move to guardianship. After the court hearing that granted the petition to move to guardianship, I went to the foster home to tell the children that they wouldn't

have to see their mother anymore. The little girl ran to me, gave my knee the biggest hug it has ever had, and said, *"Now I won't have to be afraid anymore."* Then she drew a portrait of me with beard and a huge smile on my face, which the foster mom gave to me a couple of days later. Its value to me is beyond price.

I love the title I was given, a couple of years ago: *A Real Badass*. I was caught up in a bank robbery. While I was trying to talk to the teller about needing to get into my safe deposit box, all of a sudden, I had some guy standing next to me, yelling, "*Give me all your money! Give me all your money! Give me your car keys! I'm going to stab you!!*"

Well, I found that to be quite annoying, when I was trying to talk to the teller. Turning to him, I picked up my wallet and put it in my pants pocket. Then he's yelling at me that he's going to stab me, and yells at me to give him my car keys – which I definitely was not going to do. Then he did try to stab me in my belly and up under my ribs. But the reason I was in the bank was to place two new wills that Sandy and I had just written, into our safe deposit box. They were in my coat's inside pocket; so the blade hit those folded up wills and did not penetrate my body. That was fortunate because a thrust like that could have killed me. However, a person trying to stab me makes me angry, not afraid. So when I told him I didn't have any car keys to give him, he raised his arm to stab me again. And I went after him. As I wrestled with him, he brought that blade down on my upper arm and cut me slightly. He wasn't winning the tussle with me; and just then, the teller offered him a brick of marked bills. He grabbed the money and decided to leave. He ran next door to a church parking lot where he attacked two people, injuring them, before he stole a pick-up for his getaway. He was arrested a couple of hours later.

This incident made the news; I was interviewed; and all the circles of people where I'm known, including the court system folks, had a lot of comments to make to me.

A couple of weeks later, we Community Family Court folks were all headed to a graduation of the people who had successfully completed Family Court. They would be receiving back their child from being a ward of the court, expunging all felony convictions connected to the case, and a graduation certificate. In the process, each graduating participant must make a speech to the hundred plus people in attendance. One of my dads who was graduating, said how much he appreciated me. After seeing on TV that I had attacked that bank robber, he knew that I was *"a real Badass"* who would truly protect his child no matter what; and that gave him great comfort.

Besides "Pastor," I've been called many things: The Rev, Preacher, Parson, but never "Badass." I'm really proud of that name, and what it stands for in that Dad's eyes – someone who would protect his child no matter what. I'm going to hang on to that nickname. **An aside**: That bank robber received 24 years and 10 months in prison.

I'll close with an event that took place just a few weeks before this writing. The Deputy Director for CASA of Jackson County sent me the following:

> *On Friday night, I met the maternal grand-mother of one of your prior kiddos. She is an RN in Grants Pass and when she found out that I was Deputy Director of CASA of Jackson County, she jumped into her story about you. She said, "CASAs really do make a difference, it is unbelievable." She went on to talk about how you filled so many gaps for her grand-daughter, and helped her understand what was happening with the family and the system. She said she was allowed to support her granddaughter as a grandmother and that you took the weight off of her*

with everything else. She said that her daughter and granddaughter continue to do well and that it is partly due to her CASA. She was so delighted to talk about how much you helped and said that she will be a CASA when she has a little less on her plate.

Great job George.

Other than introducing people to the healing, redeeming love of Jesus, and lifting people up in prayer to the throne of Grace, I'll gladly accept these kind words as a summation of my life of service in these times – as I reflect upon the things that I've learned along the way.

ISBN 9781075958236

Made in the USA
San Bernardino, CA
08 March 2020